Table of Contents

Colourful Lupines Grace this Cozy Fishing Cove.

Champlain's "Order of Good Cheer", from a Rare Painting by C.W. Jefferys.
Picture Division, Public Archives Canada, Ottawa (C-98232)

MARITIME HERITAGE

Our Maritime Provinces have always yielded a delicious and nutritious bounty from their waters. We have continually and successfully farmed our Atlantic Ocean, the Bay of Fundy, and Gulf of St. Lawrence, as well as our many fresh-water lakes and rivers.

Explorers, as early as John Cabot in 1497, wrote about lowering weighted baskets into the sea and hauling them up loaded with fish (probably codfish). Their catches were often so great that the weight reportedly lessened the speed of their ships.

Our Native Indians and the first settlers with their "Order of Good Cheer" had to depend upon such readily available and renewable food sources for their existence. The harvesting of our waters continues today and hopefully will withstand the ravages of varied pollutants.

We have collected the following "Down East" Maritime seafood recipes in the hope that you will enjoy sharing the treasures from our seas with your families and friends.

The Book Room takes this opportunity to acknowledge and thank everyone who very kindly contributed their recipes and helpful information which made this publication possible. A special thank you also goes to The Book Room Staff members who offered their valued assistance.

Gladys Burchell, Editor

Appetizers, Chowders and Stews

TROUT APPETIZERS

Cold:

1 to 2 cups of flaked cooked trout
1 cup of cream cheese
1 cup of cottage cheese
½ small, finely diced onion
1 tsp. paprika
dash of cayenne
1 tsp. caraway seeds
salt, pepper and butter to taste

Mix above ingredients. Serve as a spread for crackers. Great with beer.

Hot:

bulrushes
lemon juice
salt

Bulrushes may be cut in June while the blossom is still in the sheaf. Cut them near the base. Remove the top leaves and cook the reed about ten minutes in a small amount of boiling salted water. (A waterless cooker is best.) Remove outer greens and serve the inner tender stalks with a squeeze of lemon. A tasty appetizer with trout.

Joan Czapalay

SEA-FOOD DIP

1 cup chopped crab, tuna or shrimp
1 cup cream cheese
5 tbsp. mayonnaise
⅛ tsp. salt
1 tbsp. fresh lemon juice

Mix cheese, mayonnaise, salt and lemon juice to a smooth consistency. Drain seafood and add to cheese mixture. Refrigerate until ready to serve.

Mrs. G.B. Jones, Hunts Point, N.S.

PICKLE FOR SMOKING SALMON

2-3 medium sized salmon
2 quarts water
½ cup brown sugar
juice of one lemon
¼ tsp. onion salt
¼ tsp. garlic salt

Clean fish, remove heads, but leave the skin on. Cut salmon into 4″ x 2″ slabs. Marinate in above pickle for 6 to 8 hours. Remove, drain and dry. Then smoke.

Smoking Fish:

pickled salmon slabs from above
portable smoker or an old refrigerator
wood sawdust

Place fish on the shelf racks of a smoker or old fridge. Add sawdust to the bottom and ignite. Close door and smoke for approximately six hours. Check occasionally. Fish is done when browned and flaky.

Use in your favorite recipes calling for smoked fish or for hors d'oeuvres. Any other firm fish such as trout, mackerel or herring may also be used.

Mrs. Bettie M. Parker, Economy, N.S.

SOLOMON GUNDY

1 herring (salted)
vinegar
1 small onion
1 tsp. pickling spice

Clean one salt herring; remove head, fins, tail and scales. Soak overnight in cold water. In the morning drain and cut fish into ½ in. wide pieces. Place in container and cover with vinegar. Place sliced onion and pickling spice on top of fish. Set in a cool place for at least 24 hours. Serve with bread and butter. This requires no cooking, is economical and very tasty.

2-3 servings.

E.B. Higgins, Dartmouth, N.S.

LOBSTER QUICHE TARTS

Quiche Lorraine Pastry
1 egg
⅓ cup cream
  pinch of parsley
  pinch of nutmeg
  dash of Worcestershire sauce
1 lobster (cooked)
  salt and pepper
  Black Diamond cheese (white)

Line 24 tart shells with pastry (in ungreased pans). Bake 10 minutes in 450° oven. Mix beaten egg, cream, parsley, nutmeg, Worcestershire sauce, salt and pepper. Fold in finely chopped and floured lobster meat. Fill pastry shells and sprinkle with grated cheese. Bake 30 min. in 350° oven. Serve hot or cold. Shrimp may be substituted.

Makes 24 tarts.

   Roy V. Germain, Yarmouth, N.S.

SHRIMP DIP

1 (8 oz) pkg. cream cheese
1 (2½ oz) can lobster paste
1 (4 oz) can shrimp (whole or pieces)
2 tbsp. Miracle Whip
  Tabasco to taste

Mix above ingredients and refrigerate. Dip is better if made ahead of time, as it will keep for several days.

Mrs. G.B. Jones, Hunts Point, N.S.

MOCK LOBSTER SPREAD

1 lb. haddock, boiled
½ bottle chili sauce (4-5 oz.)
3 tsp. chopped pimento
1 tbsp. horseradish
½ pint sour cream
3 tbsp. mayonnaise
2 tbsp. chopped onion
2 tbsp. chopped celery

Boil 1 lb. of fresh or frozen haddock. Remove bones. Mix with remainder of ingredients. Refrigerate. Keeps for several days.

Makes 1 cup.

   Mrs. G.B. Jones, Hunts Point, N.S.

CREAMY SEAFOOD TOMATOES

½ cup cold cooked or leftover fish (haddock, cod or sole)
¼ cup chopped celery
⅓ cup mayonnaise
1 tsp. lemon juice
¼ tsp. paprika
  dash onion powder or onion salt
  salt
  pepper
  dried basil (optional)
4 medium sized fresh ripe tomatoes
4 large lettuce leaves (optional)

Remove seeds and pulp from tomatoes. Invert and drain on paper towel. Break fish into pieces insuring that all bones have been removed. Add celery, mayonnaise, lemon juice, paprika, onion powder, and salt and pepper to taste. Mix well and spoon into the tomato shells. Place each tomato on a lettuce leaf. Crush a pinch of dried basil between your fingers and sprinkle on top of mayonnaise mixture in tomato. (The herb basil complements the tomato flavour and gives this appetizer or luncheon dish a special touch.)

Serves 4 as an appetizer; 2 for a luncheon.

   Mrs. Emily Walker, Halifax, N.S.

MINCED CLAM DIP

Rub mixing bowl with clove of garlic. Soften 2 (3-ounce) pkgs. cream cheese and blend in:

1 tsp. Worcestershire sauce
1 tsp. lemon juice
  salt and pepper

Drain ½ cup minced clams. Add clams to cheese mixture with 2 tbsp. clam broth. Place in center of tray, surrounded with potato chips and crackers.

Mrs. F. Mary Tilley, Annapolis Royal, N.S.

HOT CRAB COCKTAIL SPREAD

1 (8 oz) pkg. cream cheese
1 (7½ oz) can crab meat
2 tbsp. chopped chives
1 tbsp. milk
2 tsp. Worcestershire sauce
2 tbsp. toasted slivered almonds

Thoroughly combine cream cheese, milk and Worcestershire sauce. Drain and flake crab meat. Add to cream cheese along with the chopped chives. Turn into greased 8-inch pie plate. Top with slivered almonds. Bake in 350° oven for 15 minutes, or until heated through. Keep cocktail spread warm over candle warmer. Serve with assorted crackers.

Mrs. G.M. Curry, Port Williams, N.S.

CRAB DIP

1 can crab meat or ¾ cup fresh, cooked crab
1 container of sour cream (375 ml)
1 tsp. lemon juice
dash of Tabasco sauce
⅛ tsp. paprika
⅛ tsp. onion powder or onion salt
salt and pepper
chives (optional)

Mix crab meat with sour cream, lemon juice, Tabasco sauce, paprika, onion powder, salt and pepper (to taste). Spoon into small dish and sprinkle with chopped chives. Serve with crudities (green pepper strips, cauliflower flowerets, raw mushrooms, radishes, tomato quarters, etc.), potato chips or crackers.

Mrs. Emily Walker, Halifax, N.S.

Fishing Schooners Race Home with the Catch.

CRAB SOUP

1 (10 oz) tin of tomato soup
1 (10 oz) tin of green pea soup
2 tins of homogenized milk (20 oz) or a blend of evaporated milk and 1 tin of water
1 (6 oz) tin of crab meat
Sherry (enough to soak crab meat)

Soak crab meat in sherry. Blend the above soups and milk mixture well. Heat in a double boiler and then add the crab and sherry. Delicious!

Serves 4 to 6.

Mary A. Jones, Halifax, N.S.

GOURMET STYLE FISH CHOWDER

1 quart milk
3 medium size potatoes
2 large carrots
3 celery stalks
1 small green pepper
3 medium size onions (diced)
1 cup flour
1¼ lbs. butter or margarine
1½ cups tomatoes (peeled or canned)
garlic, Worcestershire sauce
salt and pepper to taste
½ cup cheese, grated (or Cheez Whiz)
3-4 lbs. fish (haddock, pollock or cod)
shrimp or scallops (optional)

Dice vegetables to bite size pieces. Put in large bowl until needed. Cut fish into large portions. Melt butter in large pot and add flour to make a roux. Over medium heat add milk gradually to make a smooth creamy sauce. Add fish, tomatoes, cheese and diced vegetables and season to taste. Simmer over low heat for 30 minutes or until vegetables are cooked. Makes a great hearty meal for cold Atlantic weather.

Serves 6-8.

Cecilia Webb, Head Jeddore, N.S.

FLOUNDER CHOWDER

2 tbsp. butter
onions
potatoes
flounder
canned milk
pepper and salt
paprika
water

Sauté onions, coarsely diced, in 2 tbsp. butter. Add a layer of diced raw potatoes and a thick layer of flounder fillets. Sprinkle with salt and pepper after each layer. Continue until flounder is gone and then add just enough boiling water to keep from burning. When cooked, add canned milk to top layer and a lump of butter. Heat slowly. Ladle into bowls and garnish with paprika.
Number of servings depends upon layers of fish used.

Bernice G. Antrim, Parrsboro, N.S.

HADDOCK CREAM CHOWDER

1 cup celery, diced finely
1 cup onion, finely chopped
5-6 cups potato in ¼" to ½" cubes
¼ cup coarsely grated carrot
¼ cup minced fresh parsley
2 lbs. haddock fillets
1½ tsp. salt
2 cups boiling water
2 cups milk
½ pint cream or 1 small can of evaporated milk
⅛ lb. (¼ cup) butter

Using a 3 quart pot, place vegetables and fish in bottom; sprinkle salt over all. Pour boiling water over and cover, cooking at medium temperature until vegetables are tender and fish flakes readily (about 15 minutes). Break fish into small chunks. Reduce heat to low. Add milk, cream and butter. Heat thoroughly. *Do not boil.*

Yields 10 to 12 bowls.

Mrs. Jean Gordon, Milton, N.S.

6

BASIC FISH CHOWDER

2 lbs. cod or haddock
1 large chopped Spanish onion
2 large diced potatoes
  paprika
½ lb. diced salt pork
  a lot of chopped parsley
4 cups milk
8 small soda crackers, crumbled
2 tbsp. butter
  juice of 2 lemons, salt, pepper

Cut fillets in 2″ cubes. Sauté salt pork bits. Add onion and potatoes and cook until tender but not brown. Add 2 cups of boiling water and cook 3 or 4 minutes longer. Add fish and simmer 10 minutes longer. In another saucepan, combine milk, crackers, butter, salt and pepper and lemon juice. Heat just to scalding — do not boil. Combine 2 mixtures and pour into soup tureen. Sprinkle with parsley and paprika. It is even better if you substitute dry white wine for the 2 cups of boiling water.
Serves 6-8.
Mrs. Maureen Dowe, Chezzetcook, N.S.

EASTERN SHORE FISH CHOWDER

2 cups raw white fish, diced
4 cups water
3 tbsp. butter
1 cup chopped celery
2 cups raw potato, diced
4 cups milk
⅔ cup chopped onion
¼ tsp. salt
¼ tsp. pepper
¼ cup grated raw carrot
  sprinkle of parsley

Fry onions in melted butter. Add potatoes and celery. Cook a few minutes. Season well. Add cold water and cook until almost tender. Add fish and carrots. When fish is cooked, add milk. Heat to boiling point but do not boil.
Serves 6.
Kate De Baie,
Musquodoboit Harbour, N.S.

DOWN EAST CLAM CHOWDER

2 tbsp. finely diced fat, salt pork or bacon
½ cup chopped onion
1 cup diced raw potatoes
2 cups water
1 pint of clams and liquid OR canned clams (about 20 ounces total measure)
2 cups undiluted evaporated milk
½ tsp. salt
⅛ tsp. pepper

Sauté diced pork or bacon in large saucepan until crisp. Remove scraps from pan and reserve for use later as a garnish. Add onion to hot pork fat and sauté until tender. Add potatoes and water. Simmer about 10 minutes or until potatoes are tender. Add clams and liquid, milk and seasonings. Bring to simmering temperature, but do *not* allow to boil. Serve garnished with crisp pork scraps.
Serves 6.
Miss Muriel Horton, Canso, N.S.

CLAM CHOWDER TO GO

This chowder is my concoction. I was looking for a fast meal which would not only be suitable for home meals, but also for cooking on my husband's fishing and hunting trips.

1 medium sized thinly sliced onion
1 tbsp. butter or margarine
1 can baby clams
1 can potato soup
  milk or cream to cover
  seasoning salt

Melt butter in heated pot. Add onions and swirl around until onions are soft. Remove ¾ of clam juice from can. Add clams and potato soup. Stir well, then add enough milk or cream to cover ingredients. If you choose, more milk or cream can be added to thin chowder. Sprinkle lightly with seasoning salt. Stir continually until chowder is thoroughly heated.
Serves 2.
Mrs. Mary K. Watson, Dartmouth, N.S.

Removing the Catch – A Rustic Fishing Village along the Eastern Shore.

NOVA SCOTIAN CLAM CHOWDER

1 cup diced raw potato
1 medium diced onion
1 can baby clams
1 can evaporated milk
1 can lobster paste
   salt, pepper and butter to taste

Cook potato and onion in small amount of water, until done. (About 12 minutes). Add milk, clams, and lobster paste. Heat but *do not boil!* Remove from heat and add salt, pepper and a pat of butter. Serve at once, in warm bowls.

Makes 4 large servings.

   Mrs. Glen Oickle, Berwick, N.S.

EASY MANHATTAN STYLE CLAM CHOWDER

1 (10 oz) can tomato soup
1 small onion
2 small stalks of celery
1 can clams
1 cup of water
1 small potato
   salt
   pepper

Chop onion and celery; cut potato into small cubes. Add these to 1 cup of water and cook over moderate heat until vegetables are tender. Add soup, clams (including juice), and salt and pepper to taste. Simmer until heated through.

Serves 4.

   Mrs. Emily Walker, Halifax, N.S.

BASIC CLAM CHOWDER

- 2 dozen fresh clams in the shells
- ½ cup of boiling water
- ½ lb. finely chopped salt pork
- 6 potatoes, diced
- 4 onions, sliced
- 2 tbsp. butter
- 3 tbsp. of flour
- 1 tsp. of salt
- ½ tsp. pepper
- 2 qts. milk

Scrub clam shells in cold water thoroughly. Put clams in a big kettle and cover with boiling water. Cover and steam for 15 minutes. Drain the clams and save the broth. Remove the clams from the shells; cut off the hard outside of the clam, and chop. Fry salt pork for 5 minutes. Add potatoes, onion and clam broth. Cook for 15 minutes. Stir in the clams. In a separate pot, heat the butter and blend in a mixture of the flour, salt and pepper. Heat until it bubbles; then add the milk, stirring constantly. Cook for 10 minutes. Combine the two mixtures, heat quickly and serve.

Serves 8.

Mrs. Olive Roy, Halifax, N.S.

GOURMET LOBSTER CHOWDER

- ½ cup butter
- 6 medium onions, chopped coarsely
- 6 peeled potatoes, cubed
- 2 cans frozen lobster, thawed (Save the juice — it's essential)
- 1 litre whipping cream
- 1 litre blend
  - salt and black pepper
- ½-¾ cup finely chopped fresh parsley

Melt butter in a heavy pan. Cook chopped onions in butter until limp and yellow (not browned). In another pan, boil the potatoes until they are just tender — not mushy. Add potatoes and water to the onion and butter. Slice lobster into bite-sized pieces and add lobster juice, cream and blend; salt and black pepper to taste. Throw in the chopped parsley. Bring to a simmer only — do not allow to boil.

Number of servings depends on whether this is to be a starter or a main dish, and how many of the guests like lobster.

15 servings.

Mrs. Shirley Cohrs, Halifax, N.S.

MARITIME FISH CHOWDER

- ¼ lb. salt pork, cut fine
- 2 medium sized onions, diced
- 1 cup water
- 3 medium potatoes, diced
- 1 cup shrimp, diced
- 1 cup scallops, cut in quarters
- 1 cup lobster meat
- 1 cup haddock fillet, cut up
- 1 (15 oz) can evaporated milk
- 15 oz. light cream (blend)
- 1 stalk celery, diced
- 1 small green pepper, seeded and diced
- ½ tsp. thyme
  - salt and pepper to taste

In a Dutch oven, render salt pork and drain off most of the fat. Sauté the onions until transparent in 2 tbsp. fat. Add water, potatoes, celery and green pepper. Simmer until potatoes are cooked. Add fish, evaporated milk, and blend. Add thyme. Simmer until fish is cooked, about 7 to 10 minutes. Do not boil. Season with salt and pepper.

Serves 8 to 10.

Miss Ellen Ferguson, Halifax, N.S.

CHOWDERS

Fish chowders are very versatile. A thin chowder or soup makes a nourishing hot appetizer, while a thicker chowder provides a hearty luncheon or supper dish. Create your own recipes by adding a variety of your favourite chopped vegetables and fresh or left-over fish. Your experiments will prove rewarding!

SHEROSE SEAFOOD CHOWDER

- ¼ cup or more of diced salt side pork
- 1 large onion (diced)
- 1 large potato (diced)
- ½ cup celery, if desired (diced)
- 1½ lbs. haddock fillets
- ½ to 1 cup each of clams and mushrooms
- 1 can of lobster paste
- 2 or more cups milk or blend
- 1 "plop" hickory smoked or plain B.B.Q. sauce
  salt and pepper to taste
  seafood seasoning

Ingredients may be increased or decreased according to number served.

Gently cook fillets until just done. Flake. Using a heavy kettle, fry salt pork and remove scraps. Add clam and mushroom liquid to fish broth with enough water to cook diced onion, potatoes, and celery. Combine all ingredients. Thin lobster paste smoothly first with some warm milk to avoid lumping. Heat all to boiling point only. Canned fish such as salmon, shrimp, or lobster may be substituted for the clams. Sprinkle hot servings with seafood seasoning.

Serves 4 to 6.

Mary Elizabeth Snow,
Sherose Island, N.S.

FISH STOCK

When your recipe calls for poaching any fish, plan to save the broth or fish stock, for the base of a chowder or other recipe, at a later time. This stock will even freeze well until required.

PARTY IDEA

Plan to serve hot fish or seafood chowder with rolls after your bridge game or party. It's better for you than a lot of those sweets!

DELICIOUS SEAFOOD CHOWDER

- 2 medium potatoes (diced)
- 1 large carrot (diced)
- 1 large onion (diced)
- 1 lb. fresh or frozen haddock or halibut
  salt and pepper to taste
- 2 cans baby clams
- 1 lb. fresh or frozen scallops (sliced in half)
- 1 market lobster or 1 lb. shrimp (pre-cooked)
- 1½ pints blend
- ¼ cup butter
  paprika
- 3½ cups water

In a large Dutch oven, simmer potatoes, carrot, onion and halibut in water until tender. Do not drain. Add clams (do not drain), scallops and lobster, and continue to simmer for fifteen (15) minutes. Add blend; simmer until hot, but do not boil. Add butter and sprinkle with paprika. Salt and pepper to taste.

Serves 8-10.

Gayle Marie Hennessey,
Port Hawkesbury, N.S.

PIRATE'S LURE ATLANTIC FISH CHOWDER

(Often referred to as "Millionaires" Fish Chowder)

2 large onions (chopped fine)
8 tbsp. butter
2 tsp. salt
¼ tsp. pepper
½ tsp. basil
5 cups water
2 lbs. fresh lobster meat (pre-cooked)
2 lbs. fresh haddock
3 cups fresh clams (pre-steamed)
1½ lbs. fresh scallops (cut in halves)
1 package small frozen shrimp
1 large can cream-style corn
1 large can evaporated milk
6 lobster claws (full, pre-cooked and cracked)

Sauté onions in butter. Add spices and water; cover and simmer for 15 minutes. Place haddock (cut in 1 inch square pieces) and scallops in pot and simmer for 15 minutes more. Stir in corn and milk; add lobster meat (cut into small pieces), clams and shrimp. Place cracked lobster claws on top, and re-heat. Bring to hot temperature being careful to avoid scorching. Ladle chowder into large chowder bowls. Place one lobster claw on top of chowder in each bowl with initial serving.

Serves 6 with two generous portions.
Mrs. Barbara A. Low, Lr. Sackville, N.S.

CAPTAIN JOE'S SEAFOOD CHOWDER

2 medium sized potatoes
2 medium sized onions
2 lbs. haddock fillets
1 lb. scallops (cooked)
2 tins clams
2 tins mussels
1 litre homogenized milk
¼ lb. butter
salt and pepper

(if desired, lobster meat may be added)

Peel potatoes and onions and slice thinly into small pieces. Cover with water in large saucepan. Simmer until tender — about five minutes. Cut fillets in 1½ inch pieces and add. Simmer another five minutes. Add scallops, clams, mussels (and juice of same), milk, butter and lobster. Heat slowly — *do not boil.* Season with salt and pepper. Twenty-four hour refrigeration improves flavour of chowder.

Serves 6, but with the addition of more milk, and clam, mussel or other fish juices, this recipe will serve extra guests.

W.A. Moore, New Glasgow, N.S.

CHOWDER TIP

The addition of some smoked fish or oysters to your chowders will create an interesting and delicious new flavour for a change.

EEL STEW

4 lbs. cleaned eels
1 good sized turnip (diced)
3 large onions (sliced)
8 medium potatoes (cut in small pieces or quarters)
½ cup flour
salt and pepper to taste
1 tsp. dry mustard

Cut eels in 1" - 1½" pieces. Mix flour and mustard and roll eels in mixture. I put it all in a plastic bag and shake well until eels are well coated. Place eels in a stew pot. Add rest of ingredients with just enough water to see it rising — do not cover with water. Stir well. Cook for about 1 hour. You may add sliced carrots and parsnips if you like them. Either way, the stew is delicious.

Evelyn Bonn,
Musquodoboit Harbour, N.S.

TESSIE'S FISH STEW

⅓ cup butter
¾ cup finely chopped onions
1 finely chopped garlic clove
¾ cup diced celery
2 cups fresh or bottled clam juice
1 cup water
2 one-pound tins of tomatoes
¼ tsp. saffron
½ tsp. thyme
1 bay leaf (crumpled)
  salt and freshly ground pepper to taste
1 pound of cod fillets (cut into 2 inch slices)
1 pound of white fish fillets (cut into 2 inch slices)
1 pound of scallops (halved, if large)
2 small cooked lobsters or 2 cups cooked lobster meat

Melt butter; sauté onions and garlic until tender and transparent. Add celery, clam juice, water, tomatoes, thyme, bay leaf, saffron, salt and pepper. Bring to a boil and simmer for ten minutes. Add all of the white fish and scallops; cook for eight minutes or until fish flakes easily. Remove the cooked lobster meat from the shells and add to the stew. Heat thoroughly but do not overcook.

Yields 8 servings.

Mrs. Nora M. Vincent, Halifax, N.S.

STEWS

Fish stews make a great dinner on those cold wintry evenings. Busy mothers have only the one pot to fuss with. Complete the menu with a fresh tossed salad and rolls.

FISH STEW

4 slices bacon, cut in small pieces
1 large onion, chopped
3 cups diced potatoes
1 tsp. salt
½ tsp. thyme
1 bay leaf
⅛ tsp. pepper
1 (20 oz) can tomatoes
1 cup water
1 package fresh or frozen fish fillets (cod or haddock)

Fry bacon pieces; remove from pot and save for topping. Add onions and potatoes; sauté until golden. Stir in seasonings, tomatoes and water. Cover and simmer over low heat about 20 minutes. Add fish; cook 20 minutes longer. Ladle into bowls, top with bacon pieces and serve with crackers.

Sandra Irwin, Greenwood, N.S.

OCEAN OYSTER STEW

1 pint of oysters
2 cups of scalded milk
1 tbsp. of butter
  salt and pepper

Put oysters and liquid into saucepan. Heat about 6 minutes until oysters are plump. Stir oyster mixture into scalded milk. Add butter, season, and serve.

Serves 4 as a first course.

Mrs. Olive Roy, Halifax, N.S.

Sandwiches, Sauces and Salads

TUNA BUNS

1 (6 oz) tin flaked tuna
3 hard boiled eggs (chopped)
½ cup diced cheddar cheese (old)
2 tbsp. grated onion
2 tbsp. green pickle relish
½ tsp. dry mustard
    salt and pepper to taste
    mayonnaise to moisten

Combine all ingredients. Split and butter 8 hamburger rolls. Stuff with tuna mixture. Wrap individually in foil. Heat in 177°C (350°F) oven for 15 minutes. May be frozen and heated later. Excellent for cookouts.

Serves 8.

    Mrs. D.L. Chipman, Yarmouth, N.S.

OPEN-FACE FISH SANDWICHES

1 (1 lb.) can salmon or tuna (drained)
½ cup chopped celery
¼ cup sliced stuffed olives
⅓ cup mayonnaise
4 drops of Tabasco sauce
8 cheese slices
8 bread slices (toasted)
    butter

Flake fish and combine with celery, olives, mayonnaise and Tabasco sauce. Mix well. Butter the toasted bread and spread with fish mixture. Top with cheese slices. Broil only until the cheese melts, about 2 minutes.

Makes 8 sandwiches.

    Gladys Burchell, Dartmouth, N.S.

Fishermen Mending Nets, Peggy's Cove.

BAKED TUNA SANDWICHES

2 cans tuna
4 chopped hard boiled eggs
½ cup sliced olives
3 tbsp. grated onion
⅔ cup mayonnaise
½ cup soft butter or margarine, blended with 1 (5 oz) jar cheese spread
12 slices of bread

Mix tuna, eggs, olives, onion and mayonnaise. Trim crusts and butter the bread on both sides. Place six slices in a large baking dish and top with fish mixture. Cover with remaining six slices. Spread blended butter and cheese mix over the top of sandwiches. Set oven at 400° and heat sandwiches in oven for about 10-12 minutes.

Serves 6. Makes a great lunch dish or is an alternative to the "cold" sandwich. (Save the crusts and crumble when dry. Store in jar for "breading" purposes.)

Lil Shepherd, Halifax, N.S.

CRAB-BACON ROLLS

¼ cup tomato juice
1 egg, well beaten
1 (6½ or 7½ oz) can crab meat, drained and flaked
½ cup fine dry breadcrumbs
1 tbsp. chopped parsley
1 tbsp. lemon juice
¼ tsp. salt
¼ tsp. Worcestershire sauce
dash pepper
5 bacon strips

Mix above ingredients thoroughly. Place filling on 9 slices of bread. Roll up and cut in half. Pin with toothpick. Secure five strips of bacon, halved and halved again, to top of roll. Broil 5 or 10 minutes, 5 inches from heat.

Makes 18 rolls

Grace McMaster, Liverpool, N.S.

HOT CRAB MEAT PUFFS

2 egg whites, beaten stiff
1 cup mayonnaise
1 cup flaked crab meat (tuna may be substituted)
paprika
toasted buns

Fold mayonnaise and crab meat into egg whites. Season. Pile on toasted buns or toasted bread. Sprinkle with paprika and broil for 3 minutes.

Serves 4.

Mary Anne Turner, Lockeport, N.S.

SEAFOOD SANDWICH LOAF

2 (8 oz) packages of cream cheese
1 unsliced loaf of bread (whole wheat or white)

Mix first filling:
1 lb. canned tuna (drained)
½ cup chopped canned pimento
⅓ cup mayonnaise

Mix second filling:
1 lb. canned salmon (drained)
½ cup chopped celery
¼ cup chopped onion or chives
⅓ cup mayonnaise

Mix third filling:
1 lb. canned shrimp or crab meat
½ cup green pepper
⅓ cup mayonnaise

Remove crust from sides and top of bread. Slice the loaf horizontally into quarters. Butter slices and spread each of the three fillings separately. Cover with remaining slices. Mix cream cheese until fluffy and spread over top and sides of loaf. Decorate top with olives, pickles, radishes, or green pepper slices. Slice portions according to appetites.

Gladys Burchell, Dartmouth, N.S.

CREAMED LOBSTER

lobster meat (fresh or frozen)
butter
milk
flour, salt, pepper and water to taste

Boil lobsters; remove meat from shell and break into bite-size pieces. Fry lobster meat with butter in fry pan just long enough to heat through. Add enough milk to barely cover. When milk turns pinkish color, add flour, salt, pepper and water (mixed as you would for gravy) to lobster mixture to thicken. Serve on toasted buns or thick slices of toasted homemade bread.

Mary Anne Turner, Lockeport, N.S.

FISHY SANDWICH FILLING

cooked haddock
salad dressing of your choice
a few shakes of garlic salt
a bit of chopped celery
chopped onion, optional

Mix amount of haddock needed. Add salad dressing, salt, celery and onion. Mix together. Butter bread; spread fish filling. Enjoy your sandwiches with sprigs of parsley and a tossed fruit salad.

E. Carolyn Brown, Digby, N.S.

SARDINE SANDWICH FILLING

1 (3¼ oz) canned sardines
1 chopped hard boiled egg
1 small chopped onion
  lemon juice, salt and pepper to taste
¼ cup mayonnaise

Mix above ingredients well and use as sandwich filling or spread for crackers. Great as an appetizer.

Gladys Burchell, Dartmouth, N.S.

GRILLED FISH SANDWICHES

1 (1 lb.) can salmon or tuna (drained)
1 cup grated cheddar cheese
⅓ cup drained pickle relish
½ cup chopped celery
⅓ cup mayonnaise
2 tbsp. chopped onion or chives
12 slices of whole wheat bread
  butter

Flake fish and combine with cheese, relish, celery, mayonnaise and onion or chives. Mix well and spread over half of the bread slices. Cover with remaining bread slices. Brush outsides of sandwiches with butter and grill until lightly browned, 3-5 minutes.

Makes 6 sandwiches.

Gladys Burchell, Dartmouth, N.S.

Louisbourg Lighthouse – A Trusted Beacon for many Fishermen.

CREAM SAUCE MIX

1 cup flour
½ cup margarine
2 cups powdered milk
2 tsp. salt
2 tsp. pepper

Sift flour, salt and pepper. Add powdered milk and mix. Cut in margarine with blender (or use fingertips) until mixture resembles cornmeal. Store in refrigerator.

To use cream sauce with fish or casseroles, or in any recipe requiring cream or white sauce, follow this guide:
¼ cup mix + 1 cup boiling water =Thin sauce
½ cup mix + 1 cup boiling water = Medium sauce
¾ cup mix + 1 cup boiling water = Thick sauce

Add mix to boiling water. Whisk or beat briskly. Cook 5 minutes.

Anne MacAskill, Sydney, N.S.

INSTANT SHRIMP COCKTAIL SAUCE

2 tbsp. creamed horseradish
½ cup catsup
2-3 drops of Tabasco sauce

Mix horseradish into catsup. Add Tabasco, one drop at a time; taste as you go — 1 drop too much of Tabasco can make the sauce far too hot. Makes over ½ cup — would serve four shrimp cocktails. I find this sauce tastier than the commercial kind and the ingredients are always on hand.

Mrs. Emily Walker, Halifax, N.S.

QUICK TARTAR SAUCE

4 tbsp. green hot dog relish
3 tbsp. mayonnaise
    dash of lemon juice
    dash of paprika

Stir mayonnaise into green relish. Add lemon juice and paprika. (You may wish to add a bit more mayonnaise — this depends on the consistency you prefer your sauce to be.) Yields about ½ cup of tartar sauce. Perfect for those times when you need the added zest of tartar sauce to perk up sautéed or deep-fried fish.

Mrs. Emily Walker, Halifax, N.S.

TARTAR SAUCE

1 med. dill pickle
1 tbsp. capers
2 tsp. snipped fresh parsley
1 cup mayonnaise
1½ tbsp. prepared mustard
½ small onion

Chop pickle and capers as fine as possible. Cut onion into small pieces. Mix all of the above ingredients with the mayonnaise.

Approximately 2 cups.

Mrs. G.B. Jones, Hunts Point, N.S.

TUNA CRUNCH SALAD

1 (6 oz) tin tuna
¼ cup chopped green pepper
1 tbsp. minced onion
1 cup crisp cabbage, shredded
½ cup salad dressing
2 tbsp. vinegar
2 cups potato chips

Flake tuna; add pepper, onion, cabbage and mix well. Mix salad dressing and vinegar together and fold in just before serving. Add potato chips and toss lightly. Serve on crisp lettuce.

6 servings.

Evelyn Bonn,
Musquodoboit Harbour, N.S.

MOLDED TUNA FISH SALAD

2 (6 oz) cans of tuna chunks
2 chopped hard boiled eggs
½ cup chopped stuffed green olives
1 small minced onion
2 tbsp. capers
1 envelope plain gelatine
¼ cup cold water
2 cups mayonnaise or boiled dressing

Drain and flake tuna. Combine with eggs, olives, onion and capers. Soak gelatine in cold water 5 minutes. Dissolve over hot water and add to dressing as you stir constantly. Mix thoroughly with fish mixture. Turn into ring mold and chill until firm. Unmold on a bed of lettuce. Fill center with tomato and egg wedges, and red onion rings.

Serves 8.

Mrs. Robert W. Coupland,
Bridgewater, N.S.

JELLIED SALMON LOAF

1 tbsp. gelatine
¼ cup cold water
½ cup chopped celery
¾ cup mayonnaise
1 cup cooked salmon, flaked
¼ cup chopped stuffed olives
½ tsp. salt (or to taste)
¼ tsp. paprika (or to taste)
1 cup cooked peas (if desired)

Soak the gelatine in the cold water. Dissolve it over hot water and add to mayonnaise which has been warmed. Fold in other ingredients. Mold and chill. Serve with tossed salad.

Serves 8-10.

Mrs. R.M. Johnson, Scotch Village, N.S.

Sandwiches, Sauces and Salads

SALMON — CUCUMBER SALAD

6 (5½ oz) cans salmon
2⅔ cups salmon liquid
5⅓ oz unflavored gelatine
8 cups boiling water
2 cups lemon juice
4 cups mayonnaise
4 cups sour cream
2 tsp. salt
1 cup finely chopped onion
4 cups finely chopped celery
4 cups finely diced cucumber
1½ cups finely chopped pimento

Drain salmon, reserving liquid. Break salmon into bite-size chunks and crush bones. Soak gelatine in salmon liquid. Add boiling water and stir to dissolve gelatine. Combine lemon juice, mayonnaise, sour cream and salt. Stir in dissolved gelatine and chill. Combine salmon, onion, celery, cucumber and pimento. Fold fish mixture into gelatine mixture and pour into 2 oiled pans (18″ x 12″ x 2½″). Chill until firm. Cut each pan into 25 servings. Serve on crisp lettuce with slices of tomato.
Serves 50.
Anne MacAskill, Sydney, N.S.

LUNENBURG COUNTY CUCUMBER SALAD

4 medium sized cucumbers
1 (½ pt.) tub sour cream
4-5 tbsp. of vinegar
3-4 tbsp. sugar (to taste)
1 medium sized onion
½ tsp. salt

Peel cucumbers and slice thinly into a deep bowl. Sprinkle with ½ teaspoon salt. Put a weight on top and leave for 2 or 3 hours at room temperature. Drain off juice, and rinse lightly. Add thinly sliced onion, sour cream, vinegar, sugar and a shake or so of pepper. Marinate in fridge for an hour or longer. Serve with fresh salmon or trout. *Serves 8.*
B. Burchell, Dartmouth, N.S.

SALMON IN CUCUMBER ASPIC

1 envelope plain gelatine (1 tbsp.)
¼ cup cold water
½ cup boiling water
1½ tsp. salt
1 tsp. sugar
2 tbsp. lemon juice
1 tbsp. vinegar
dash freshly ground black pepper
12 oz. cucumber, peeled and finely grated
1 lb. can of red salmon
lettuce
mayonnaise (preferably homemade)

Soften gelatine in cold water for 5 minutes. Add boiling water and stir until dissolved. Add salt, sugar, lemon juice, vinegar and pepper. Cool and then add cucumber with its juice. Chill until slightly congealed, stirring occasionally. Remove and discard skin from salmon; crush the bones and flake the fish. Fold into gelatine mixture. Place in lightly oiled mold (about 1 qt.) and chill until firm. Unmold on glass serving dish lined with lettuce. Serve with mayonnaise.
Serves 4.
Mrs. Nora M. Vincent, Halifax, N.S.

MOLDED SHRIMP SALAD

2 pkg. gelatine
¼ cup cold water
1 (250 ml) bottle Thousand Island Dressing
1 (7 oz) can broken shrimp
½ cup finely chopped celery

Soak gelatine in cold water for five minutes. Dissolve over low heat. Add remaining ingredients. Pour into mold and chill until firm. Note: If serving with crackers as a dip, use 1 pkg. gelatine.
Serves 4.
Enid Murray, Sydney, N.S.

FISH MOLD

2 envelopes gelatine
⅛ cup cold water
½ cup hot water
2 tbsp. lemon juice
  salt and pepper
1 tbsp. salad oil
1 bottle stuffed olives
½ green pepper (cut in strips)
2 (7 oz) cans tuna (salmon or crab may be substituted)
1 cup mayonnaise
1 tbsp. malt vinegar
½ cup tomato ketchup
1 tbsp. onion juice
2 tbsp. celery (chopped)
1 tbsp. green pepper (chopped)
1 (7 oz) can of shrimp

Coat fish mold with oil; lay sliced olives for scales. Use ½ olive with pimento for eyes. Lay green pepper for tail. Line sides of mold with shrimp. Soften gelatine in cold water and then dissolve in hot water, lemon juice, salt and pepper. Place all ingredients including gelatine and any left over olives in a blender and blend. Pour into fish mold. Chill until set. Invert on a platter for serving; garnish with fresh parsley.

Joanne Turner, Dartmouth, N.S.

LOBSTER SALAD

1 (12 oz) tin of frozen or cooked lobster
¼ cup finely chopped onion (optional)
½ cup finely chopped celery
1 tbsp. chopped green pepper
1 tbsp. chopped parsley
½ tsp. tarragon
1 cup pure mayonnaise
  white pepper to taste

1 tsp. lemon juice or white wine for added flavour
  leaf lettuce

Place above ingredients in a bowl and blend well. Serve on a bed of leaf lettuce with tomato and hard boiled egg slices.

Serves 4.

Mrs. Ruth Frank, Dartmouth, N.S.

ORIENTAL SALAD

This salad is quite attractive and can be used as a centerpiece in salad buffet luncheons. Ideal for working ladies or gentlemen as it can be prepared prior to a party.

1 (10 oz) pkg. frozen peas
1 (5-6 oz) pkg. minute rice
2 pkg. frozen shrimp
1½ cups chopped celery
¼ cup chopped onion

Cook peas, rice and shrimp per directions. Cool. Then add following ingredients to above:

Dressing:

½ cup salad oil
3 tbsp. cider vinegar
2 tsp. curry powder
1 tsp. salt
1 tbsp. soya sauce
½ tsp. Accent
½ tsp. sugar
½ tsp. celery salt
½ cup slivered almonds
  tangerines for garnish

Mix all above lightly. Don't mash. Refrigerate several hours or overnight. Add slivered almonds and tangerines just before serving.

Serves 12-14.

Shirley Hines, Head of Chezzetcook, N.S.

Casseroles

DELUXE TUNA CASSEROLE

1 (400 g) pkg. deluxe macaroni and cheese prepared as directed

Mix:

1 (10 oz) can of cream celery soup
1 (10 oz) can of cream cheese soup
½ can of water (5 oz.)

Add above to macaroni and cheese.

Add:

1½ cups frozen peas
2 (7 oz) tins of tuna chunks, drained and coarsely broken
1 small jar chopped pimento
potato chips

Crush potato chips and sprinkle over top of ingredients. Bake uncovered in 375° oven for 45 minutes, or until bubbly. Note: No salt is added as soups provide plenty.

Serves 6-8.

Mrs. Robert W. Coupland,
Bridgewater, N.S.

TANGY SALMON CASSEROLE

1 (15½ oz) can salmon
3½ cups medium noodles
¼ cup mayonnaise
2 (16 oz) cans French cut green beans
2 tbsp. flour
1 tsp. grated onion
½ tsp. pepper
1 cup sour cream
½ lb. natural old cheddar cheese

Cook noodles in boiling water until tender. Drain. Mix noodles with mayonnaise. Place in a greased 10" x 11½" baking dish. Flake salmon and spread over noodle mixture. Melt butter in saucepan and gradually stir in dry ingredients and grated onion. Add sour cream and stir until well blended. Drain beans and add to the sauce. Pour over salmon and noodle mixture. Cover with cheese. Bake 350° degrees for 20 to 25 minutes.

Serves 4-5.

Rachel Forbes, Dartmouth, N.S.

SALMON CASSEROLE SUPREME

1 large can of salmon or 1½ lbs. fresh salmon
6 medium potatoes, cooked, cooled and sliced
2 sliced hardboiled eggs
1 large sliced onion
1 small green pepper
salt and pepper to taste
large piece of butter
½ cup flour
1½-2 cups milk

Place a layer of potatoes on bottom of 1½ qt. casserole. Add a layer of salmon and some of each vegetable. Repeat until all is used up. Cover with the following white sauce: Melt a large piece of butter in a saucepan and add ½ cup flour. When mixed well, add 1½ cups milk. If you like a thinner sauce, use 2 cups of milk. Add eggs, salt and pepper to taste. Cook for 5 minutes then pour over fish and vegetables. Sprinkle with bread crumbs and bake in 375° oven for half an hour.

Serves 4 or 5.

Evelyn Bonn,
Musquodoboit Harbour, N.S.

SALMON OR TUNA CHEESE CASSEROLE

1 lb. salmon (or tuna) with liquid
½ cup finely diced celery
1½ cups bread crumbs
2 beaten eggs
1 cup grated cheese
1 tbsp. lemon juice
1 tbsp. minced onion

Flake fish in a bowl, removing all bones. Add all ingredients and mix thoroughly. Bake in 350° oven for one half hour or in a slow cooker for 2 to 3 hours.

Serves 4.

Deian Hartwell, Shearwater, N.S.

CODFISH PIE SUPREME

2 lbs. fresh cod (1 kg)
6 tbsp. butter
5 tbsp. flour
3¾ cups milk (900 ml)
3 tbsp. grated cheese
   salt and cayenne pepper
1½ cups un-cooked rice
1 small onion
1 tbsp. curry powder

Cook fish; drain and break into small pieces. Melt 3 tbsp. butter; stir in flour and cook 3 minutes. Pour in milk and stir until smooth and thick. Add cheese, salt and pepper. Simmer 5 minutes with lid on. Cook rice in salted water. Rinse in cold water to separate grains. Melt 3 tbsp. butter in pan; fry onion; add rice, curry and salt. Stir constantly until rice is lightly browned. Pack rice mixture into casserole dish; add cod and cover with cheese sauce. Place in 300° oven to reheat when required.

Note: A little soya sauce may be added before serving.

Serves 4-6.

Mrs. Nancy J. Ferguson, Spryfield, N.S.

SHREDDED CODFISH CASSEROLE

1 lb. or 2 cups of freshened, cooked salt cod (see Helpful Hints)
2 cups mashed potatoes
½ cup milk
2 eggs, beaten
¼ cup melted butter, or other fat
2 tbsp. chopped onion
   salt and pepper to taste

Flake salt cod. Mix all ingredients together and season to taste. Place in a greased 1½ quart casserole, and bake in a moderate oven (350°) for 30 minutes or until set.

Makes 4 to 5 servings.

Mrs. R.G. Hann, Halifax, N.S.

Having been Cleaned, Split, and Salted, These Fish Lie Drying in the Sun.

HADDOCK BAKE

2 lbs. haddock fillets (approximately)
¼ cup butter
¼ cup chopped onion (can be increased)
¼ cup diced celery
½ tsp. salt
½ tsp. thyme
2 cups soft bread crumbs
1 or 2 tomatoes

Grease baking dish — loaf style pan accommodates the fillets nicely. Melt butter in fry pan, and sauté onion and celery until tender. Add salt, thyme and bread crumbs, and toss well. Place half of the fillets ("shiny side" down) in dish, and cover with half the sautéed dressing. Add pieces of chopped tomato. Repeat with second layer of fillets, dressing and chopped tomato. Melt a small quantity of extra butter to pour over top; then bake at 450° for 10 minutes per inch thickness. (This includes dressing thickness.)

Serves 4, and can be readily adapted for more by increasing ingredients and size of dish used.

Lil Shepherd, Halifax, N.S.

BAKED BUBBLY FILLETS

1 lb. any fresh or frozen fish fillets
1 (10 oz) can cream of mushroom soup
2 tbsp. chopped onion
1 tbsp. lemon juice
3-4 tbsp. water
½ cup grated old cheese
chopped red and green pepper (optional)

Place frozen fillets of your choice in individual casserole dishes (or one shallow one). Place soup, onion, lemon juice and water over fillets. Sprinkle with grated cheese. A little chopped green or red pepper adds colour. Bake at 375° for 20-30 minutes. Do not overcook.

E. Carolyn Brown, Digby, N.S.

HADDOCK FILLETS CASSEROLE

1 lb. haddock fillets
4 buttered soda crackers
1 can chicken with rice soup
¼ cup tomato ketchup
¼ cup Carnation milk
½ cup water

Separate strips of fillets. Place a thick strip in the bottom of a casserole dish. Over this, spread the crackers and the soup. Over all spread the ketchup and pour on the milk and water. Bake uncovered in a moderate oven (350°F.) for about 30 minutes.

Serves 4.

Miss Janet E. Winsloe,
Murray Harbour, P.E.I.

"ALMOST-CRAB" CASSEROLE

2 lb. haddock fillets
¼ cup butter
4 tbsp. flour
2 cups milk
2 tbsp. salad oil
1 cup sour cream
salt and pepper
1 cup sharp, shredded cheddar
½ lb. fresh sliced mushrooms
1 small minced onion
frozen peas, or 1 (10 oz) can peas

Cover haddock fillets with water and simmer gently for 15 minutes. Drain and break fish into large chunks. While poaching fish, melt butter and blend in flour. Add milk and cook over low heat, stirring constantly, until thick. Add cheese, and cook until cheese melts. Remove from heat. Sauté onion and mushrooms in oil for 5 minutes. Add to cream sauce. Then add the cooked peas, sour cream and flaked fish. Mix carefully. Salt and pepper to taste. Using a shallow 3 qt. baking dish, heat in moderate oven until bubbly and lightly browned on top.

Serves 6 to 8.

Miss D. Walker, Dartmouth, N.S.

Casseroles

WHITE FISH CASSEROLE

3 tbsp. butter or margarine
1 medium green pepper, cut fine
2 tbsp. flour
1½ cups milk or cream
1 cup fish, flaked (cod, haddock or halibut)
½ cup soft bread crumbs
½ tsp. salt
½ tsp. pepper
½ cup sherry (optional)
2 cups potato chips (crushed)

Cook green pepper in margarine or butter until soft. Stir in flour and blend until smooth. Add milk or cream; cook and stir until thick. Add flaked fish, bread crumbs, salt, pepper and sherry. Mix until ingredients are blended. Put in a casserole dish and cover with crushed potato chips. Bake at 375° for 30 minutes.

Serve with the following sauce:
1 (10 oz) can mushroom soup
½ can water

Blend and heat; then pour over casserole portions.
Serves 6.
Anne MacAskill, Sydney, N.S.

SMOKED FILLET CASSEROLE

1 lb. smoked fillet
6 medium potatoes
3 tbsp. flour
3 tbsp. butter or margarine
1 tsp. salt
½ tsp. pepper
1 cup milk, or more, to cover fish
¼ cup diced onion
paprika (optional)

Slice 3 potatoes thinly and place in casserole dish. Add remainder of ingredients, except milk. Cover with remaining 3 sliced potatoes. Pour in milk until it nearly covers all the potatoes. Sprinkle paprika over top, if desired. Bake in moderate oven (350°) until done (about 1½ hour).
Serves 6.
Miss Muriel Horton, Canso, N.S.

SMOKED FILLETS IN WHITE SAUCE

2 lb. of smoked fillets
water

Wash 2 lb. of smoked fillets. Cook ½ hour in fresh water. Save liquid. Cut fish into serving-sized pieces and place in casserole dish. Cover fish with white sauce (below) and bake in 325° oven for ½ hour.

White Sauce:
2 tbsp. butter
2 tbsp. flour
1 cup of water from fish
1 cup canned milk
salt and pepper

Melt 2 tbsp. butter. Add 2 tbsp flour, stir in 1 cup of water from fish and 1 cup canned milk. Season with pepper and salt. Heat until thick, stirring constantly.
Serves 6.
Betty Hardiman, Port Hawkesbury, N.S.

CHICKEN HADDIE CASSEROLE

1 can chicken haddie
2 onions
2 tbsp. butter or margarine
2 hard cooked eggs
2 cups bread crumbs
3 cups milk, or more if necessary
1 tsp. celery salt
salt and pepper to taste
2 tbsp. chopped parsley
cornstarch to thicken

Sauté onions. Add chicken haddie, milk, salt and pepper to taste, and celery salt. Simmer for 5 or 10 minutes; then add cornstarch and parsley. Cook until mixture starts to thicken; then place in casserole. Top with sliced hard boiled eggs. Sprinkle the bread crumbs over all and dot with butter or margarine. Place in 350° oven until bread crumbs turn golden brown — about 30 to 40 minutes. Serve with mashed potatoes.
4 to 5 servings.
Mrs. Maureen Power,
Musquodoboit Harbour, N.S.

LOBSTER PIE

This recipe was created for a family of four so they could enjoy this rather expensive delicacy at a moderate price.

   5 tbsp. butter
   ¼ cup sherry
   1 cup cooked lobster meat (packed) and reserved liquid
   ¾ cup thin cream
   1 tbsp. flour
   2 egg yolks

Add sherry to 2 tbsp. melted butter. Boil 1 minute. Remove from heat and add ¾ cup cream and lobster. Set aside. Melt 3 tbsp. butter, add flour and cook until it bubbles. To the drained liquid from lobster add 2 beaten egg yolks; add both to flour mixture. Put in double boiler and cook until thick. Place all ingredients in casserole. Sprinkle with topping below.

Topping: Mix and blend well:
   ¼ cup cracker crumbs
   ¼ tsp. paprika
   1 tbsp. finely crushed potato chips
   1½ tbsp. Parmesan cheese
   2 tbsp. melted butter

Bake 15 minutes in 300° oven.

Makes 4 large servings.

Mariam J. Clifford, Tiverton, N.S.

SEAFOOD PILAF

   ¾ cup uncooked long grain rice
   1 (10½ oz) can condensed chicken with rice soup
   1 (4½ oz) can shrimp, drained
   ¼ cup dry white wine
   2 tbsp. butter
   1 (3 oz) can sliced mushrooms (⅔ cup)
   1 (7½ oz) can crab meat, drained, flaked and cartilage removed
   1 tbsp. minced onion

In a skillet, brown rice in butter for about 5 minutes. Add mushrooms with liquid and remaining ingredients. Turn into 1½ qt. casserole. Bake covered for 55 minutes in 350° oven. Fluff with fork and bake uncovered for 5 minutes more.

Serves 6.

Rachel Forbes, Dartmouth, N.S.

Fishermen Make-ready to Set Out in the Early Morning Fog at Tiverton.

LOBSTER SUPREME

1 cup lobster meat
1 cup mushrooms (sautéed)
½ cup chopped celery
½ cup chopped onion
¼ cup green pepper
½ tsp. salt
1 tsp. Worcestershire sauce
½ cup salad dressing
1 cup white sauce
  grated cheese

Combine first six ingredients and mix well. Add Worcestershire sauce, salad dressing and white sauce (see below). Pour into lightly greased 1½ qt. casserole. Sprinkle lightly with grated cheese. Bake at 350° for 30 minutes.

White Sauce:

2 tbsp. butter
2 tbsp. flour
½ tsp. salt
  dash of pepper
1 cup milk

Melt butter in saucepan. Add flour, salt and pepper. Cook over low heat until smooth. Remove from heat and stir in milk. Cook 1-2 minutes longer, stirring constantly. Serve with Germanian Rice.

Germanian Rice:

4-6 cups prepared Uncle Ben's long-grained or wild rice
1 (10 oz) can mushrooms
1 onion (chopped)
1 (10 oz) can consommé soup
  butter

Prepare rice according to package instructions and place in a casserole dish. Brown the mushrooms and chopped onion in butter. Add to rice; then add the can of undiluted consommé soup. This may be prepared in advance and heated in oven when ready to serve. Bake in 350° oven for approximately ½ to ¾ hour.

Serves 4 to 6.

Mrs. Sharen K. Goulden, Shelburne, N.S.

DEVILLED SEAFOOD

2 lbs. haddock fillets
1 lb. lobster (cooked)
8 tbsp. butter
9 tbsp. flour
1 cup evaporated milk or cream
1½ cups fresh milk
2 tbsp. cornstarch
1 tbsp. lemon juice
1 tbsp. Worcestershire sauce
4 tbsp. ketchup
1 tbsp. horseradish
1 clove garlic (grated)
1 tsp. prepared mustard
½ tsp. salt
1 tsp. soya sauce
1 tsp. Accent
4 tbsp. minced parsley
½ cup sherry
  bread crumbs

Put fillets in double boiler, cover and steam for 20 minutes. When cool break into bite-sized pieces. Separate lobster into small pieces. Melt butter in a large pan and blend in flour. Add evaporated milk and fresh milk to flour-butter mixture slowly. Stir and cook until slightly thick. Add a little milk to cornstarch and add that to milk mixture. Stir and cook for 15 minutes. Add lemon juice, Worcestershire sauce, ketchup, horseradish, garlic, mustard, salt, soya sauce and Accent. Mix and stir in parsley and sherry. When mixed add fish and lobster and press into greased pan. Top with bread crumbs and dots of butter. Bake ½ hour in 400° oven. (This can be prepared the day before and stored in fridge. Bring to room temperature before baking.)

Serves 10.

Enid L. Germain, Yarmouth, N.S.

LOBSTER SCALLOP

1 lb. cold-pack lobster
⅔ (400 g) pkg. macaroni, uncooked
1 cup chopped celery
½ cup chopped onion
½ cup green pepper, slivered
1 (10 oz) can cream of chicken soup
½ (10 oz) can cream of tomato soup
½ cup milk
1 (10 oz) can mushroom pieces
2 tbsp. Cheez Whiz
  buttered crumbs

Break up lobster; cook macaroni and simmer vegetables in small amount of water until tender. Combine soups, milk and mushrooms, including liquid. Add cheese and combine all ingredients. Pour into buttered casserole and top with crumbs. Bake in 350° oven 50-60 minutes.

Serves 4 to 5.

Rachel Forbes, Dartmouth, N.S.

SCALLOP CASSEROLE

1 lb. scallops
½ cup chopped scallions
1 (10 oz) tin sliced mushrooms
Sprinkle above with salt and pepper.

Add:
½ cup white wine or ½ cup water

Bake above ingredients in casserole in 325° oven for 25 minutes.

While baking, prepare sauce:
1½ cup homogenized milk
¼ cup butter
½ cup grated old cheese
1 tbsp. flour
  salt and pepper

Stir and blend until smooth and thick. Add sauce to casserole and bake an additional 15-20 minutes.

Serves 4.

Betty Hardiman, Port Hawkesbury, N.S.

DEVILLED CLAMS

2 cups clams
½ cup clam liquid
2 tbsp. minced onion
2 tbsp. each of minced green pepper and celery leaves
¼ cup chopped celery
4 tbsp. butter
½ tsp. pepper
½ tsp. prepared mustard
¾ cup cracker crumbs

Chop clams fine and simmer in their own liquid for 5 minutes. Cook onion, green pepper, celery and leaves in melted butter until tender. Mix all ingredients together and bake in a casserole at 350° for 20 minutes.

Serves 4.

Bettie M. Parker, Economy, N.S.

MUSSEL CASSEROLE

4 lbs. fresh mussels
6 tbsp. butter
  few grains nutmeg
2 tbsp. Worcestershire sauce
2 tbsp. flour
1 cup mussel broth
1 cup cream
4 egg yolks
  salt and pepper
1 cup coarse bread crumbs
  butter and paprika

Wash and steam mussels until shells open. Save the broth. Melt butter; add nutmeg, Worcestershire sauce and flour. Mix well and stir in 1 cup of mussel broth. Stir and mix until smooth and thick. Remove from heat and stir in cream. Beat egg yolks; add to sauce. Add salt and pepper. Return mixture to stove; heat to boiling point but *do not boil.* Pour into a casserole and add mussels. Cover with bread crumbs, dot with butter and sprinkle with paprika. Bake at 450° for 15 minutes.
Serves 6.

Evelyn Bonn,
Musquodoboit Harbour, N.S.

PARTY FISH CASSEROLE SUPREME

This is a very adaptable recipe — ideal for dinner parties, because it can be made beforehand and popped into the oven when guests arrive.

1½ lbs. fish

One or more kinds of fish or shellfish may be used, depending on the occasion and the pocketbook. Whitefish: sole, haddock, cusk or turbot. Shellfish: scallops, lobster or shrimp. Our favourite fish combination is haddock and scallops.

Sauce:

    3 tbsp. butter or margarine
    3 tbsp flour
1¼ cups milk
    2 tbsp. mayonnaise
    2 tbsp. dry sherry
    2 tbsp. chopped parsley
    ½ tsp. grated lemon peel
       salt and pepper to taste
       paprika

Melt butter and stir in flour; add milk. Cook, stirring until mixture boils and thickens. Add mayonnaise, sherry, parsley, lemon peel, salt and pepper. Arrange fish in a single layer in shallow ("oven to table" style) baking dish. Pour sauce over fish and dust with paprika. Bake in 375° oven for about 30 minutes.

Serves 4-6.

   Mrs. Susan K. Lally, Halifax, N.S.

SHELLFISH NOVA SCOTIAN

½ cup butter
6 tbsp. flour
4 cups milk
4 tbsp. minced onion
1 tsp celery salt
¼ tsp. grated orange rind
2 tbsp. minced parsley
2 tbsp. minced green pepper
2 tbsp. minced pimento
    dash Tabasco
4 tbsp. sherry
2 eggs, beaten
2 tsp. salt; dash of pepper
6 cups chunked cooked lobster meat
2 cups large shrimp (cooked and cut up)
½ cup bread crumbs
2 tbsp. melted butter

Melt ½ cup butter in double boiler. Add flour; stir and add milk. Cook until thickened. Add onion, celery salt, orange rind, parsley, green pepper, pimento, and Tabasco. Remove from heat and add sherry. Stir some sauce slowly into beaten eggs and then return to remainder of sauce. Add salt, pepper and shellfish. Place all in a large casserole. Sprinkle with crumbs mixed with melted butter; bake at 350° for 20 minutes. Serve with plain or wild rice on the side.

Serves 10-12 people. (May be increased by adding more shellfish.)

   Mrs. E.M. Wrathall, Dartmouth, N.S.

SEAFOOD SUPREME

2 tbsp. butter
2 tbsp. flour
1 cup milk
¼ tsp. salt
¼ tsp. curry powder
2-3 tbsp. chopped green pepper
1 (7 oz) can of each: tuna, crab meat, shrimp
1 (10 oz) can mushrooms
buttered bread crumbs
paprika

Make a medium white sauce with butter, flour, milk and salt. Season with curry powder and green pepper. Blend sauce with tuna, crab meat and shrimp. Add mushrooms. Put in a baking dish or scallop shells. Top with buttered bread crumbs and dust with paprika. Bake at 325° for 20 minutes.

Serves 6.

Mary B. Green, New Glasgow, N.S.

FISH DISH FOR TEN

Make sauce:
1 cup mushrooms
8 tbsp. butter
8 tbsp. flour
4 cups milk
¼ cup sherry
¼ tsp. salt
1 tsp. dry mustard
dash of Tabasco

Steam for 15 minutes:
1½ lbs. scallops
1½ lbs. fresh haddock
2 cans lobster or crab

Pour sauce over fish in shallow baking dish. Add buttered bread crumbs on top. Bake in 350° oven for 45 minutes.

Serves 8-10.

Mrs. F. Mary Tilley, Annapolis Royal, N.S.

SUPPER FISH DISH

1 pkg. of shell macaroni (cooked)
(5-6 oz) can of each: lobster, crab meat, shrimp
1 (10 oz) can cream of celery soup
Small amount of each: onion flakes, grated cheese, margarine
8 crackers (broken into small pieces and crumbled)

Alternate a few layers of macaroni shells with fish and add a few onion flakes. Pour undiluted soup over the above. Sprinkle with crackers, grated cheese and dots of margarine. Bake until brown, at 350°F. Serve with tossed salad and hot biscuits.

Serves 6-8 people.

Mrs. R.M. Johnson, Scotch Village, N.S.

SEAFOOD CASSEROLE

2 lbs. fresh haddock
1 lb. fresh scallops
Meat from 1 large cooked lobster, or 1 tub cold packed lobster
2 boxes fresh mushrooms
grated cheese
bread crumbs
rich cream sauce (recipe below)

Rich Cream Sauce:
½ cup butter
½ cup flour
2 pints cream
½ cup white wine

Steam haddock and scallops about 5 minutes. Add lobster and mushrooms, stirring gently. Add cream sauce. Put in casserole with crumbs and cheese on top. Bake in 350° oven for about ½ hour. Serve on toast triangles with baked potato, green salad and dry white wine.

Serves 6.

Mrs. F.A. Dobson, Ellershouse, N.S.

Cleaning the Catch.

FISH CASSEROLE SUPREME

  1 lb. white fish fillets
½ lb. scallops
  2 (10 oz) cans shrimp soup
  1 (10 oz) can cream of chicken soup
  1 cup milk (more if needed)
  2 cans oysters
1½ cups rice
  1 can of lobster or 2 cans of lobster
    paste
  1 (10 oz) can cream of mushroom
    soup
  1 large can of salmon
1½ cups bread crumbs
  4 tbsp. butter

Place fish fillets and scallops in saucepan and cover with milk and some water. Cook slowly for 8 minutes. Drain and reserve liquid to use as sauce. To the liquid add cans of soup along with liquid from cans of fish. Put all ingredients together and stir. Grease casserole and put the mixture in. Spread crumbs and butter on top and bake in 350° oven for 1 hour. Boil and strain rice. Keep warm. Serve casserole over rice. Great for buffet or fish dinner.

Serves 10-12.

  Mrs. M.D. Brennan, Dartmouth, N.S.

SUPER SEAFOOD CASSEROLE

  2 cups chopped onions
  3 cups chopped celery
  3 tbsp. butter
  1 tsp. salt
¼ tsp. pepper
  5 cups milk
¾ cup all purpose flour
½ cup butter
  1 lb. sliced pasteurized cheese
10 oz. lobster meat
½ lb. crab meat
¾ lb. cooked shrimp
  1 lb. cooked scallops, quartered

Sauté onion and celery in 3 tbsp. butter, salt and pepper. Meanwhile, bring milk to boil; mix in butter and flour; add celery, onion and cheese. Cook until cheese is melted and sauce slightly thickened. Add cooked seafoods and place in large casserole or individual casseroles. Heat until bubbly and brown in a moderate oven.

Serves 4-5.

  Rachel Forbes, Dartmouth, N.S.

Casseroles

SEAFOOD SCALLOP

1 lb. fresh fish fillets
1 lb. scallops
1 qt. milk
1 large tin of lobster
2 tins oysters or clams
  crab meat and shrimps (optional)
1 (10 oz) can mushroom soup
½ cup of flour
6 tbsp. butter
1½ cups bread crumbs
3 cups cooked rice
½ tsp. Worcestershire sauce
2 tbsp. sherry
  bread crumbs

Place fillets and scallops in saucepan; cover with milk and cook slowly about 8 minutes. Drain and reserve milk for sauce. Blend flour and butter; add reserved milk gradually. Add mushroom soup, juice from lobster, sherry and Worcestershire sauce. Stir constantly over medium heat until thick. Butter a large casserole. Pour in layer of sauce, add layer of cooked rice, add layer of fillets, and other seafoods. Repeat with alternate layers of sauce, rice and fish mixture, ending with cream sauce. Sauté bread crumbs in butter in frying pan. Cover seafoods generously with bread crumbs. Heat in 350° oven for one hour.

Serves 6-8.

Rachel Forbes, Dartmouth, N.S.

FISH FOR BREAKFAST

For a delicious change, treat your family to kippers or smoked fish for breakfast or brunch. This fish may be poached or baked with a little butter and pepper in a moderate oven. Serve with poached eggs, toast and lemon wedges. An English tradition to start your day!

HISTORICAL NOTE

Cape Breton was named by French fishermen who sailed from Brittany, France. They came during the summer months to catch and dry codfish. The French were followed by the English, Biscayan, Basque, Spanish and Portuguese fishermen who made summer stations on the Nova Scotia coast.

DELUXE FISH CASSEROLE

1 can of frozen lobster or 1 lb. freshly cooked lobster (shelled)
1 small bag of frozen shrimp
½ lb. scallops
1-2 lbs. haddock fillets
¼ lb. butter or margarine
3-4 tbsp. flour
1 (385 ml) can of evaporated milk
  salt and pepper to taste
1 tsp. paprika
¼ tsp. mace
½ tsp. M.S.G. or Accent
1 tsp. sugar
  bread crumbs

Cook scallops and haddock in just enough salted water to cover fish. Drain and save the water. In the top of a double boiler mix melted butter or margarine with flour. Slowly add the water from the fish and milk. Blend until sauce is a good thickness for casserole. If necessary add a little extra blend or milk. Season the sauce with salt, pepper, paprika, mace, M.S.G. or Accent and sugar. Chop fish and place into a casserole dish and pour the sauce over all. Cover with bread crumbs and dot with butter. Bake in moderate oven for 30 minutes.

Serves 8-10.

Mary A. Jones, Halifax, N.S.

SOUNDS GREAT.

Main Courses

BAKED HALIBUT — YARMOUTH STYLE

1½-2 lbs. halibut (1 piece, preferably the tail)
  small onion
2 bay leaves
  roux of melted butter, flour, salt and pepper

Remove black skin from halibut. In a suitable baking pan, place a slice or two of onion and a couple of bay leaves. Add the fish with white skin down. Make a roux of melted butter, flour, salt and pepper. Spread over the fish. Bake in hot oven (400°) until fish separates easily from bone. Don't overcook. Serve with a Hollandaise sauce *(See Hollandaise Sauce Recipe page 46)* or a mayonnaise mixed with lemon juice and chopped pickles.

Serves 6-8.

  Margaret Ayer, Lindsay, Ontario

INDIVIDUAL HALIBUT STEAKS — BAKED IN FOIL

  halibut steaks
  potato slices
  leftover frozen or canned vegetables
  butter
  salt and pepper

Tear off a piece of foil wrap for each halibut steak. Place steak on foil. Put one serving of potato slices and one serving of vegetables on steak. Season with salt, pepper, and a piece of butter. Bring sides and corners of foil up and close together tightly so juices don't escape. Bake on the oven rack at 375° for approximately 45 min. or until potatoes are tender.

Serve in the foil – no dishes or pots to clean.

  Mary Anne Turner, Lockeport, N.S.

BROILED HALIBUT STEAK

2 lbs. halibut steak
½ cup soya sauce
¼ cup catsup
½ cup chopped fresh parsley or 2 tbsp. parsley flakes
½ cup orange juice
2 tbsp. lemon juice
½ tsp. minced garlic
1 tsp. pepper

Combine ingredients well together and pour sauce over fish. Allow to marinate for 1 hour. Place fish on broiler rack about 4 inches from broiler element. Cook 8 to 10 minutes on each side. Baste frequently with sauce while cooking.

Serves 4-6.

  Rachel Forbes, Dartmouth, N.S.

BAKED HALIBUT STEAKS

  halibut steaks, cut 1 inch thick
2 tbsp. lemon juice
¼ cup melted butter or margarine
  pepper and salt to taste
1 cup buttered bread cubes
  parsley

Cheese Sauce:

2 tbsp. butter or margarine
2 tbsp flour
  dash of paprika
½ tsp. salt
1 cup milk
½ to 1 cup grated cheese

Place halibut steaks in a greased baking dish. Add lemon juice, melted butter, salt and pepper. Cook sauce in double boiler; then pour over halibut steaks. Spread 1 cup buttered bread cubes on top and sprinkle with parsley. Bake fish in hot oven (400°). For fresh fish allow 10 minutes per inch thickness; frozen fish allow about 20 minutes per inch.

Servings depend on size and number of halibut steaks.

  Mrs. Olivette A. Zinck, Lunenburg, N.S.

The Live Lobster is a Dark Greenish-brown in Colour.

LOBSTER À LA NEWBURG IN THE SHELL

2 boiled lobsters (medium size, or 1 big one)
1½ oz. butter or margarine
¼ pint white wine or cider
3 yolks of egg
½ pint cream (or milk)
  salt and pepper
  cayenne

Have the lobster halved. Remove the intestine (that is the dark line running throughout). Save the shell halves. Remove all flesh and cut it up. Melt butter in saucepan; add lobster and pour wine over all. Beat the eggs with cream or milk and add to the lobster. Season with salt, pepper and cayenne. Heat quickly, but on no account let it boil. Fill the empty lobster shell halves with the mixture. Dot with a little butter or margarine. Place under broiler to brown quickly. For larger amounts, brown in a hot oven. Serve piping hot.

Serves 4.

Margaret Poulton, Dartmouth, N.S.

DIGBY LOBSTERS

1-1½lb. live lobster (per person)
  salt to taste
  onions
  celery
  green pepper
  carrots

Fill a large kettle with water and salt to taste. Heat water to boiling point. Plunge lobsters, head first, into the water. Cover kettle and let return to boiling. Then, remove the cover and cook for 10 minutes for 1 lb. lobsters, or 15 minutes for 1½ lb. ones. *Do not overcook* because the lobster meat will become tough. Remove lobsters from the kettle; save the water which drains from the lobsters. This can be used with the empty shells as the base for soup or sauce.

Soup:

Add onions, celery, green pepper, and carrots to the reserved liquid and cook for 30 minutes.

E. Carolyn Brown, Digby, N.S.

SCALLOPED LOBSTER

1½ cups lobster meat
1 cup soft bread crumbs
1 cup thin cream
1 egg, well beaten
2 tbsp. melted butter or margarine
½ tsp. prepared mustard
few drops onion juice
½ tsp. salt and pepper, if desired
crumbs for topping

Mix in order given. Put into greased baking dish and cover with buttered crumbs. Bake 30 minutes in moderate (350°) oven. Note: Crab meat, fresh or canned, may be substituted for lobster meat.

Serves 4.

Mrs. Janice Sampson, Dartmouth, N.S.

CAPE BRETONER'S LOBSTER DELIGHT

1 pkg. fresh mushrooms
2 medium onions
1 large can tomatoes
1 large can tomato paste
½ cup red table wine
1 (4 oz) bottle of pimento
  liquid from lobsters
  sweet basil
  cumin seed
  tarragon
1 garlic clove
8 small lobster tails

In a large pot, fry mushrooms, onions and crushed garlic. Pour off butter. Mix in tomato paste and tomatoes. Add wine, pimentos, liquid and spices. Simmer for 1 hour. Add meat from lobster tails and a few shells for additional flavour. Simmer 1 hour longer and remove shells before serving.

Serves 3.

Susan Murchie, Halifax, N.S.

Delicious Lobster, Cooked and Ready-to-serve.

HALIBUT — COUNTRY STYLE

2 lbs. halibut steak (1 inch thick)
½ tsp. salt
⅛ tsp. pepper
½ cup finely chopped onion
½ pint dairy sour cream

Season steaks with salt and pepper and place in a shallow, greased baking dish. Cover with finely chopped onions. Spread with sour cream. Bake uncovered in moderate oven (350°) for 30 minutes.
4-6 servings.

Muriel Horton, Canso, N.S.

BAKED ORANGE HALIBUT STEAKS

2 pkgs. (about 12 oz each) frozen halibut steaks
¼ tsp. salt
¼ tsp. grated orange peel
½ cup orange juice
2 tbsp. chopped parsley

Place frozen halibut steaks in a single layer in a shallow baking dish. Sprinkle with salt and orange peel; pour orange juice over fish. Bake in moderate oven (350°), basting once or twice with juices in dish, for 30 minutes, or until fish flakes easily. Place on a heated platter; garnish with parsley.
Serves 4.

Sandra Irwin, Greenwood, N.S.

BAKED HALIBUT SUPREME

lbs. halibut
1 tsp. lemon juice
1 cup milk
½ cup cracker crumbs
2 tbsp. butter; salt, pepper
2 tbsp. green pepper or pimento

Place halibut in buttered baking dish. Brush with lemon juice and add milk. Sprinkle with salt, pepper, pimento or green peppers. Cover with cracker crumbs. Dot with butter. Bake 1 hour in 350° oven.
Serves 4.

Enid L. Germain, Yarmouth, N.S.

BAKED HADDOCK — LUNENBURG STYLE

2 lb. fresh haddock fillets
1 large onion (sliced)
1 cup milk
1 tbsp. butter
1 tbsp. flour
3 pieces salt pork, sliced thin (optional)

Place haddock fillets in a greased baking dish and put pieces of salt pork on fillets. Cover with salt, pepper, butter, milk and sliced onion. Sprinkle flour over fish and bake in hot oven (375°) occasionally basting while baking. (About 45 min.)
Makes 4 servings.

Janice M. Knickle, Lunenburg, N.S.

DRESSED BAKED HADDOCK

1 whole haddock — cleaned, scaled and rinsed in cool water
2 onions
1 cup water
1 shredded wheat biscuit (crushed)
1 slice dry bread or 1 cup croutons
1 egg
salt and pepper to taste
1 tsp. oregano
¼ lb. butter

Dressing:
Mix together shredded wheat biscuit, croutons or bread, salt, pepper, half of the butter, 1 onion (minced or cut fine), and oregano. Add one egg; then set aside.

Dry haddock with paper towel. Place dressing in body cavity and close with skewers and string. Place fish in pan; add salt and pepper. Dot with butter and add sliced onion. Add 1 cup water. Bake at 325° for 1 hour. Before serving, thicken juice in pan with 1 tablespoon of flour, and serve as a sauce.

Serves 4-6.

Mrs. Thomas Hardiman,
Port Hawkesbury, N.S.

FRESH STUFFED HADDOCK WITH ORANGE STUFFING

5 lbs. fresh haddock (whole)
2 qts. chicken stock
2 sliced lemons
thickly sliced onion
2 cups semi-dry white wine

Stuffing:

stale French bread
grated orange rind
2 tbsp. of orange juice or more to taste
sage, oregano, salt and pepper to taste
2 chopped king crab legs
minced onion

Make the stuffing and fill the fish. Close fish with skewers. Place fish in a large deep electric fry pan (or a Dutch oven), filled with chicken stock and wine. Place lemons and onion on top of the fish. Cover and cook 10 minutes at 390°; then reduce heat to 100°. Let the dish sit covered for 20 minutes at this temperature. Do not overcook. Remove fish. Boil stock until it reduces to half. Make a sauce by adding salt and pepper to the thickened broth.

Serves 6.

Linda MacLellan, Halifax, N.S.

BAKED HADDOCK IN FOIL

3-4 lbs. whole fresh haddock (or halibut)
2 onions
5-6 slices of side bacon
juice and grated rind of 1 lemon
paprika
tin foil

Clean fish. Lay it on a large piece of heavy tin foil on cookie sheet. Slice onions in rings and cover fish with them. Lay strips of bacon on top of onion slices. Sprinkle juice and grated rind of lemon on top of bacon strips. Then sprinkle paprika on top of bacon. Fold tin foil to seal fish. Bake in a 425° oven. After 20 minutes, fold back tin foil and return to oven for another 15 minutes to crisp bacon and finish cooking fish. Garnish fish servings with onions and bacon.

Serves 6.

Mrs. Gloria Mader, Halifax, N.S.

THE FISHERMEN'S WAY

1 lb. haddock fillets
butter
cream
pepper

Place frying pan with tight fitting cover on a cold burner and add haddock fillets. Put 2 or 3 tablespoons butter on top of fish; cover pan and heat slowly on low to medium temperature. Never use "hot" as this fish is not fried. Check in about ½ hour, then add a little cream and freshly ground pepper. This is delicious if done properly.

Makes 2 servings.

Enid L. Germain, Yarmouth, N.S.

SAUCY BAKED HADDOCK

1 lb. frozen haddock fillets (cod may also be used)
1 (10 oz) can cream of celery soup (undiluted)
½ onion (chopped)
1-1½ tbsp. lemon juice
1 tsp. salt
½ tsp. pepper
½ tsp. Italian seasoning

Place frozen block of fish in a slightly oiled 9" x 6" baking dish. Combine the other ingredients and spread over fish. Cover. Bake at 350° for 45 minutes (or until done).

Serves 4-6.

Mrs. R.M. Johnson, Scotch Village, N.S.

Picturesque Village near Yarmouth Provides Lobster, Tuna and Deep-sea Fishing.

BAKED HADDOCK FILLET AU GRATIN

1-1½lb. haddock fillet
- 1 tsp. salt
- 1 tsp. onion salt or 1 small chopped onion
- 1 tsp. pepper
- ¼ cup Parmesan cheese
  enough milk to cover fish in dish

Cut fillet in medium size pieces; dip in flour and place in buttered 8″ x 8″ pan. Sprinkle with salt, pepper, onion and Parmesan cheese. Add enough milk to cover fish. Bake at 350° for 30-35 minutes.

Serves 4.

Mrs. Sharen K. Goulden, Shelburne, N.S.

GEFILTE FISH PATTIES

- 2 lbs. haddock fillets
- 1 small carrot (peeled)
- 2 eggs
- 1 onion
- ¼ tsp. garlic powder
- ½ cup bread crumbs (or matzo meal)
- ¼ cup cold water
  salt and pepper (to taste)
- 1 tbsp. sugar
- ¼ tsp. paprika

If using a food processor, cut vegetables and mince 10 seconds on steel blade. A grinder could also be used. Add other ingredients and process one minute or until very smooth. Put mixture in bowl and refrigerate for 1 hour. Heat skillet with an amount of Mazola oil (¼″ in pan). Make fish patties with moist hands and roll in bread crumbs. Fry on each side until golden brown (3-4 minutes). Patties can be eaten hot or cold. They will also freeze well.

Mrs. Shirley Burnstein, Halifax, N.S.

SCALLOPED HADDOCK

deep scallop shells

2 lbs. Duchess potatoes (recipe below)

1½ lbs. smoked haddock fillets

1¼ pints milk

1¾ oz. butter or margarine and

1¾ oz. flour, made into Basic White Sauce with the milk used to cook haddock

3 oz. Parmesan cheese or grated cheddar

1 oz. extra butter

pepper to taste

Duchess Potatoes:

2 lbs. boiled potatoes, dried well after boiling

2 oz. butter

2 egg yolks

salt and pepper

Beat in butter and egg yolks whilst potatoes are still hot. Season.

Cut haddock into 3″ - 4″ pieces. Cover with milk and cook over low heat until fish is tender (10 minutes). Strain and use milk, flour and butter to make Basic White Sauce. When cooled, skin haddock and flake fish lightly with finger tips. Fold into sauce and stir in 2 oz. cheese, and pepper if desired. Place Duchess potatoes in icing bag and pipe a fat border around rim of each scallop shell. Fill center of shells with haddock and sauce mixture.

Sprinkle top surfaces with remaining cheese. Dot with small pieces of butter and cook at 400° for 20 to 25 minutes, depending on size of shells.

If using large ones allow 1 shell per serving. If shells are small allow 2 per serving.

Margaret C. Poulton, Dartmouth, N.S.

BARBECUED MACKEREL

Since mackerel is an oily fish, it is especially delicious broiled or barbecued. To barbecue, split and open fish flat. Baste with sauce of ¼ cup vinegar and ½ cup brown sugar. Double wrap with heavy weight tin foil. Barbecue for approximately 15 min. on each side, turning carefully. Open tin foil and continue cooking if you prefer to have fish crispier.

BAKED FRESH TUNA WITH TOMATO SAUCE

6 slices of fresh tuna (about 4 to 6 oz. each)

½ tsp. black pepper

1 tsp. salt

¼ tsp. nutmeg

1½ cup chicken stock

1 tsp. softened butter

¼ tsp. dried oregano

juice of one lemon

2 tbsp. finely chopped fresh or dried parsley

1½ cup tomato sauce to which 1 tsp. white sugar has been added (sugar helps remove bitterness from sauce.)

tinfoil

Preheat oven to 350° F. Place tuna slices in a baking dish and pour the chicken stock over all. Sprinkle with salt and pepper. Butter a piece of tinfoil and place securely over top of baking dish with buttered side down. Bake for 15 minutes, basting occasionally. When fish flakes, remove slices from baking dish with a slotted turner and set aside on a warm platter. Pour the juices from the baking dish into a saucepan and boil down to make ¾ cup of liquid. Add tomato sauce with sugar, oregano and nutmeg, and simmer until hot. Add lemon juice. Pour this sauce over tuna slices and sprinkle with fresh parsley.

Serves 6.

Mrs. Ruth Frank, Dartmouth, N.S.

MARINATED PAN-FRIED TUNA

4 fresh tuna steaks (1" thickness)
2 tbsp. cooking oil
2 tbsp. chopped fresh parsley
1 small finely chopped onion
   pinch of thyme
   juice of 1 fresh lemon
   salt and pepper to taste
½ cup cooking oil for frying

Soak tuna steaks for 1 hour in marinade of oil, parsley, onion, thyme, lemon juice, salt and pepper. Drain fish and roll steaks in a little flour. Heat fry-pan with ½ cup of cooking oil to medium temperature. When pan is heated, add tuna steaks and fry on both sides until you can flake fish with a fork. Serve with tartar sauce or lemon wedges. (Note: Fresh tuna does not freeze well; fresh tuna should be dark red in colour.)
Serves 4.
   Mrs. Ruth Frank, Dartmouth, N.S.

BROILED SWORDFISH STEAKS

4 fresh swordfish steaks (about 2 lbs.)
1 tsp. salt
¼ tsp. black pepper
   paprika to taste
⅓ cup melted butter or margarine
1 tbsp. lemon juice
   fresh parsley

Wash and dry fish steaks. Rub steaks with salt, pepper and paprika. Arrange fish in a shallow baking dish and spread on half of the lemon and butter mixture. Broil for about 10 to 12 minutes. Turn steaks, spread on the remainder of lemon and butter mixture, and broil for another 10 to 12 minutes. Remove swordfish steaks to a hot platter, garnish with fresh parsley and serve with a fresh tossed salad. (Additional suggestion: Mash hot potatoes until fluffy. Add one beaten egg and ½ tsp. baking powder. Pop under the broiler for a few minutes.)
Serves 4.
   Mrs. Ruth Frank, Dartmouth, N.S.

NOVA SCOTIAN SOLE DISH

1½ lbs. fresh fillet of sole (½"-¾" thickness)
1½ tsp. oil
   juice of a fresh orange or lemon
½ cup butter (melted)
   parsley flakes, pepper, salt (dash)
   grated rind of either orange or lemon

Cut fish into five inch long portions. Prepare baking dish with the oil and place fish in dish, making sure it absorbs the oil. Pour juice over fish. Then add melted butter, salt, and pepper. Finally add parsley and grated rind. Bake for 12-15 minutes at 375°. Serve with broccoli and boiled potatoes. Looks and tastes great. *Serves 4.*
   Barbara J. Turner, Dartmouth, N.S.

FILLETS OF SOLE À LA CINDY

4 fillets of sole (or more if desired)
   shrimp pieces (broken bits are less expensive than whole)
1 (10 oz) can mushroom soup and small amount milk
1 green pepper — chopped, not too fine
6-8 fresh sliced mushrooms
1 chopped onion
   small amount cooking oil
   parsley flakes
   celery salt

Heat mushroom soup, to which the milk is added, stirring occasionally. Meanwhile, sauté green pepper, sliced mushrooms and onion in fry pan. When browned, add to mushroom soup mix. (If you wish to add extra shrimp to this mix too, you may do so.) Place shrimp bits on each fillet; roll up and place in baking dish. Pour soup mixture over all; season lightly with parsley flakes and celery salt. Bake in 350° oven for 20 to 30 minutes or until fish flakes.
Serves 4. (Six fillets, plus increased ingredients, will serve 6; and so on.)
   Lil Shepherd, Halifax, N.S.

BROILED FILLETS OF SOLE WITH GRAPEFRUIT

2 lb. fresh sole fillets
1 small grapefruit
  salt and pepper to taste
6 tbsp. melted butter or margarine

Wash fillets and then dry them on a paper towel. Arrange fish in a baking dish, spread with melted butter, and sprinkle with salt and pepper. Peel grapefruit and divide it into sections. Arrange sections on top of sole fillets and broil for about 15 minutes, keeping fish about 6 inches from broiler elements.

Serves 4.

Mrs. Ruth Frank, Dartmouth, N.S.

SOLE WITH CASHEWS

4 medium fillets of sole
  (approximately 1½ lbs.)
⅓ cup of raw cashews (available at health food stores)
¼ cup butter or margarine
2 tsp. of lemon juice
  salt and pepper

Sprinkle fillets with lemon juice, salt and pepper. Melt the butter in a skillet. Add cashews and, stirring frequently, sauté the cashews until they are light brown. Remove the cashews from the pan with a slotted spoon. Set them aside for the time being. Lay the sole fillets in the pan. If you feel it necessary, you may wish to add more butter at this time to prevent the sole from sticking to the pan. Sauté until the fish flakes with a fork. Watch carefully. It is very important not to over or undercook the fish. Turn once and remove when done. Arrange the sole on a warmed serving platter and sprinkle with cashews. Pour warmed butter and juices from the pan over all. Sweet, crunchy cashews add a delicious contrast in taste and texture. This is very good served with hot boiled rice and a green vegetable or salad.

Serves 4.

Mrs. Emily Walker, Halifax, N.S.

BAKED STUFFED SOLE

2 lb. fresh sole fillets
1 large onion (chopped)
¼ cup melted butter
1 cup fresh bread crumbs
  green onions
  lemon slices
  summer savory

Place sole fillets in a well buttered, rectangular casserole dish. Cover deeply with dressing (see below). Top with more fillets. Dot well with butter, green onions (snipped) and thin slices of lemon.

Dressing:

Sauté chopped onion in ¼ cup melted butter. Add summer savory and cook over low heat until onions are soft. Toss with 1 cup fresh bread crumbs until well coated.

Bake at 350° for ½ hour. Serve with Hollandaise Sauce. *(See Hollandaise Sauce Recipe on Page 46.)*

Serves 4.

Enid Murray, Sydney, N.S.

SALMON LOAF WITH EGG SAUCE

Remove skin and bones from a 1 lb. tin of salmon or 2 cups of fresh fish. Drain and flake salmon saving the liquid. Add 2 slightly beaten eggs to fish and mix well. Stir in:

- 1 tbsp. finely minced onions
- 1 tbsp. green pepper or parsley (chopped)
- 1 tsp. lemon juice
- ½ tsp. salt
- ⅛ tsp. pepper
- ½ cup milk and liquid from fish
- 2 cups Special K cereal

Mix above ingredients well and pour into well greased 9″ x 4½″ loaf pan. Bake in moderate oven (350°) for 45 minutes.

Serve with Egg Sauce:

- 4 tbsp. butter
- 2 tbsp. flour
- salt and pepper to taste
- 1 cup milk
- 1 hard boiled egg
- 1 tsp. lemon juice

Heat 2 tbsp. butter, flour and seasonings stirring constantly until smooth. Add 1 cup of milk and cook slowly for 5 minutes. Add 1 tsp. lemon juice and two more tablespoons of butter — a little at a time. Finally add one thinly sliced hard cooked egg. Heat thoroughly.

Serves 4-6.

Mrs. Charles Sutherland, Halifax, N.S.

BARBECUED SALMON

Season fresh salmon with salt, pepper, dots of butter and chopped fresh chives. Double wrap a whole piece of salmon or individual steaks with heavy weight aluminum foil. Barbecue for approximately 15 to 20 minutes on each side. Turn carefully without tearing foil so that salmon continues to cook in its own juice. Check for doneness until fish flakes.

STEAMED FRESH ATLANTIC SALMON

- 4 lbs. fresh Atlantic salmon
- parsley

Wrap the salmon in cheese cloth. Place a rack in bottom of heavy pot and place the salmon on top of rack. Add 2 or 3 cups of water to pot. Cover and steam for ½ hour or more until it tests done. (A thin pot requires more cooking than a heavy one.) Remove salmon from rack and remove skin. Place on fish platter; decorate with fresh parsley. Serve with egg sauce and cucumber salad. I also serve steamed parsley potatoes and carrots to make a very colorful dish.

Egg Sauce:

Make a basic cream sauce with:

- 4 tbsp. butter
- 4 tbsp flour
- 2 cups milk
- salt and pepper
- chopped fresh chives

Add 2 or 3 hard cooked eggs, chopped quite fine. Serve hot.

Should serve 8.

B. Burchell, Dartmouth, N.S.

SMOTHERED SALMON

Necum Teuch family recipe since late 1800.

- 2 lbs. fresh salmon
- 1 medium sized onion
- 1 tbsp. butter
- salt and pepper
- thickening

Cut salmon in one inch steaks; place in heavy pot or Dutch oven. Cover with cold water; add cut-up onion, salt and pepper. Bring to boil; then simmer gently for 30 minutes. (Lift salmon from pan to platter.) To the juices in the pan, add butter; then thicken the gravy. Pour over the salmon on platter while piping hot. Serve with mashed potatoes and peas.

Serves 4.

Mrs. Foster S. Levy, Halifax, N.S.

SALMON QUICHE

- 1 can (about 8 oz) salmon
- 2 cups (½ lb.) grated cheddar cheese
- 2 tsp. grated onion
- 1 tbsp. all purpose flour
- ¼ tsp. salt
- 3 eggs
- 1 cup milk
- 1 unbaked 9″ pastry shell

Drain salmon; remove skin and bones. Flake fish. Combine cheese, onion, flour and salt in bowl; fill pastry shell with alternate layers of salmon and cheese mixture. Beat eggs and milk in bowl; pour over salmon-cheese layers in pastry shell. Bake in very hot oven (450°) 15 minutes; reduce heat to slow (325°) and bake 30 minutes longer or until firm in centre.

Serves 6.

Sandra Irwin, Greenwood, N.S.

The Atlantic Salmon – One of the Most Sought After Game Fish.

BAKED SALMON OR HADDOCK ROLL

2 cups flaked, cooked salmon or haddock (approx. 1 lb. and canned may be used)
1 egg
1 tbsp. white sugar
½ tsp. salt
1 tsp. dry mustard
1 tbsp. sherry (or 1 tbsp. vinegar)
1 cup milk
1 cup cracker crumbs
1 cup cooked macaroni
½ cup finely grated carrots

Drain fish and remove skin and bones. Flake. Beat egg slightly; add sugar, carrots, salt, mustard, sherry, milk, ½ cup cracker crumbs, fish and macaroni. Shape into an oblong roll and chill. Before baking gently roll fish mixture in reserved ½ cup crumbs. Baste with 1 tablespoon of salad oil. Place on trivet in roaster and bake in moderate oven, uncovered, until thoroughly heated. Serve with tomatoes and cucumbers.
Serves 6.
Mariam Clifford, Tiverton, N.S.

SISSIBOO SMELTS

12 fresh smelts
bread crumbs
2 oz. butter
salt and cayenne pepper to taste
lemon juice and wedges
parsley

Wash and dry, cleaned fish thoroughly in a cloth. Arrange them in a flat baking dish. Cover with fine bread crumbs and dot with butter. Season and bake for 15 minutes in a 400° oven. Just before serving add squeezed lemon juice and garnish with fresh parsley and lemon wedges.
Serves 4.
Geraldine Ellis Gates, Weymouth, N.S.

SOLE ACADIA

2 lbs. sole — filleted (any white fish fillets may be substituted)
1 orange
¼ cup butter
1 tbsp. flour
salt and pepper
¼ cup grated cheddar cheese
chopped parsley
few orange slices

Grate rind of orange, squeeze juice and make up to ⅔ cup with water. Melt butter in pan and add orange rind. Sauté this for 2 minutes. Add fish, flesh side down, and fry gently for two minutes; turn fish and continue to fry for five minutes. Put fish in oven-proof dish and keep warm. Stir flour in remaining butter in pan. Stir in orange juice. Bring to boil, stirring constantly. Season and simmer for 2 minutes. Lower heat and add ⅔ of cheese, stirring until melted. Pour sauce over fish, sprinkle with remaining cheese and grill until brown and bubbling. Garnish with parsley and orange slices.
Serves 4.
Mrs. Edith Myers, Dartmouth, N.S.

CREOLE FILLETS OF SOLE

1 medium size onion (chopped)
½ cup chopped celery
4 tbsp. butter or margarine
1 (8 oz) can tomato sauce
½ tsp. salt
½ tsp. curry powder
⅛ tsp. pepper
1 cup chopped green pepper
2 pkgs. (1 lb. each) frozen fillets of sole, partly thawed

In a skillet, sauté onion and celery in butter or margarine until soft. Stir in tomato sauce, salt, curry powder, pepper and green pepper. Cut fish in serving-size pieces; place in single layer in sauce in skillet. Cover and heat to boiling. Then simmer about 25-30 minutes, or until fish flakes easily. Serve with cooked rice, carrot sticks and peas.
Serves 6.
Sandra Irwin, Greenwood, N.S.

WEST INDIAN STYLE COD WITH SEASONED RICE

1 oz. cooking oil
3 lbs. fresh cod fillets
1 can stewed tomatoes (drained with juice saved)
3 stalks of celery
3 medium onions
1 small green pepper
1 tsp. ginger (ground)
2 tsp. garlic powder
2 tbsp. sugar
1 tsp. curry powder
salt and pepper to taste

Fry onion, celery, green pepper and tomatoes in oil over low heat. Add spices and fish and simmer over low heat for twenty minutes in a covered pot. Serve with rice.

Seasoned Rice:

2 cups Uncle Ben's long grain rice
3½ cups water
2 chicken bullion cubes
1 tbsp. salt
¼ lb. butter
2 tbsp. garlic powder
3 tbsp. curry

Bring spices and water with left-over tomato juice to boil. Add rice and butter. Then reduce heat to lowest setting and let set for 45 minutes to 1 hour. Don't remove lid from pot until ready, then stir rice. Serve fish on bed of seasoned rice.

Serves 6-8.

James J. O'Brien, Head Jeddore, N.S.

COD AU GRATIN

2 lbs. grated cheddar cheese (or ⅔ parts cheddar and ⅓ Mozzerella)
3 lbs. fresh cod fillets
¼ lb. butter
1 cup flour
1 quart milk
salt and pepper to taste
½ fresh lemon
1 small onion
3 tbsp. vinegar

Poach cod in salt, water, vinegar, lemon and onion. Drain. Place milk, salt and pepper in boiler and bring to a slow boil. Melt butter and add flour in a saucepan to make a roux, or thickening agent. Add roux to boiling milk until it becomes a very thick sauce. Cook at a slow boil for 10 minutes. Grease a baking pan and add fish. Cover with sauce. Grate cheese and sprinkle over the top of the fish. Place in hot oven at 400-450° and bake until crust is a golden brown. This is a very rich and tasty dish.

Serves 4-6.

James J. O'Brien, Head Jeddore, N.S.

ACADIAN COD FISH DISH

1½ lbs. of salt cod bits
egg sauce (recipe below)

Soak codfish in cold fresh water overnight. In the morning drain water; put fish in a pot and add cold water. Bring to boil and let simmer for half an hour. Then drain the water off. Put in a serving dish and add egg sauce.

Egg Sauce:

2 cups milk
4½ tbsp. flour
salt and pepper to taste
1 tbsp. of butter
4 hard boiled eggs

Place milk in saucepan over medium heat. Gradually add flour. When thick, add salt and pepper, butter and eggs. Pour over fish. Serve with potatoes and vegetables of your choice.

Serves 4.

Cathy Theriault, Annapolis Royal, N.S.

Fish Weir, Seen Here at Low Tide, is Completely Covered at High Tide.

BAKED STUFFED SHAD

Shad has been traditionally fished in the Bay of Fundy. They are caught in brush weirs resembling a tall fence, erected on the ocean floor a distance from shore. Shad come in with the tide and become entangled in the weir. At low tide, they are picked off by hand. In bygone days a man with horse and buggy drove out to the weir and kept moving as they worked to avoid being mired in the soft mud of the ocean floor. The season is mid-summer. A first-time shad eater should be warned that they have a great many double pronged bones. An old hand handles this slight inconvenience with aplomb and declares it the finest flavour in the world.

1 whole freshly caught shad, about 1 kilo (2-2½ lb.)

Stuffing:

3 cups (750 ml) stale bread crumbs
1 small onion, chopped
2 tbsp. (30 ml) chopped parsley
1 tbsp. (15 ml) summer savoury
1 egg and milk to moisten
salt, pepper

— — —

4 strips bacon
3 tbsp. (45 ml) melted fat

Scale and clean freshly caught fish. Cut off head, tail, and fins. Wash thoroughly in cold water. Remove backbone and large bones with a sharp knife, if desired. Mix stuffing; fill fish cavity, and sew, tie or skewer shut. Place whole fish in suitable covered casserole, containing the melted fat. Lay 4 bacon strips over the fish. Bake covered at 350° for 40 minutes per kilo. (15 minutes per pound.) Serve with baked potatoes and greens.

Makes 4-5 servings.

Mrs. E.T. Goring, Maccan, N.S.

SAUCY COD

Traditional. A salt cod recipe from the Atlantic ocean around the Cape of Good Hope, South Africa. Early Dutch settlers in Nova Scotia had Malay slaves who introduced spicy flavours to the Dutch kitchens.

1 lb. salt cod
3 medium potatoes (unpeeled)
4 medium tomatoes
3 tbsp. oil
3 medium onions, thickly ringed
½ tbsp. fresh chopped hot chilies or ¼ tbsp. dried, crushed chilies
1 tsp. minced garlic
1 tbsp. brown sugar
1 lemon
parsley

Soak cod in fresh water for at least 12 hours, gently squeezing cod and changing water every 4 hours. Cook potatoes, uncovered until almost tender; then peel and cut into 1 inch cubes. Place tomatoes briefly in boiling water to loosen skins; pierce and peel; slice into rounds. In a heavy skillet, heat oil, add onions, and sauté until lightly browned; add tomatoes, chilies, garlic and sugar. Cook briskly until most of the liquid has evaporated and mixture is thick enough to hold its shape lightly. Stir in cod and potatoes. Reduce heat to low and cover tightly. Simmer for 20-25 minutes, or until cod flakes easily. Taste for seasoning. Serve at once on rice topped with chopped parsley and wedges of lemon. Homemade pickles go well with this dish.

Serves 4.

Valerie Hearder, Lunenburg, N.S.

CREAMED SALT CODFISH

1 medium-sized codfish (salted)
3 tbsp. melted butter
2 tbsp. flour
1 cup milk
1 tsp. chopped parsley or chives

Shred the fish and soak it overnight in fresh water. Drain when ready to use, and shred again evenly. Mix flour and melted butter with cod. Stir in milk slowly and blend until smooth, keeping heat low. Continue stirring constantly until thickened as desired. More milk may be added if necessary. As a finish, sprinkle chopped parsley or chives over the top. This may be served on mashed potatoes or wedges of toast. Creamed salt cod is a real Maritime delicacy.

Serves 4.

Gertrude E. Inness, Porter's Lake, N.S.

SALT COD AND PORK SCRAPLINGS

1 lb. or more of dried salt cod
potatoes, cooked with peelings left on
small amount of salt pork
onions

Fish may need to be soaked in fresh water overnight, or simmered with water changed until only salty enough for your taste. Poach fish approximately ½ hour or until it flakes with fork. Fry onions with pork until pork is crisp and shrinks in size. Boil potatoes until done and serve with fish. Pour the onions and pork scraplings over fish and potatoes.

Serves 2-3.

Arita King, East Petpeswick, N.S.

DEEP FRIED CODFISH BALLS

4 large potatoes (cooked)
1 cup shredded dried salt cod (soaked in fresh water overnight)
1 heaping tsp. of butter
1 beaten egg
  salt and pepper to taste
  fat for deep-frying

Dry out potatoes and fish for ½ hour and then mash fish and potatoes together. Add the butter, the well-beaten egg, salt and pepper and mix well. Dip out spoonsful of the mixture and shape into balls. Place in frying basket and immerse in heated deep fat until nicely browned. Drain on paper towelling.

Serves 4-6.

Mrs. Maureen Dowe, Chezzetcook, N.S.

TARRAGON PLAICE OR TURBOT

3 lb. turbot or plaice fillets
2 tbsp. margarine
  salt and pepper to taste
  tarragon to taste, yet liberal
2 cups medium cheddar cheese
2 sliced medium sized fresh tomatoes

Place fish in shallow pan greased with margarine. Season with salt and pepper to taste. Sprinkle with liberal amount of tarragon. Add finely grated medium cheddar cheese. Top with sliced tomatoes. Bake in moderate oven (325°) for 20 minutes until fish is flaky. Serve hot from the oven with rice or potato and green vegetables.

Serves 6.

Cecilia Webb, Head Jeddore, N.S.

DEEP FRIED FISH

1 lb. haddock, cod or sole
⅔ cup flour
5 tsp. baking powder
¼ tsp. salt

Cut fish into one or two inch portions. Add enough water to flour, baking powder and salt to make a very thick, globby paste (batter). Dip each portion of fish in batter to coat all over. Deep fry at 390° for 3 minutes only. Turn each piece after 1½ minutes to brown evenly.

Serves 5.

Joanne Turner, Dartmouth, N.S.

STUFFED FILLETS OF FLOUNDER

2 lbs. fillets of flounder
  bread crumbs
  oysters, asparagus, lobster or sardines
  lemon juice
  salt and pepper

Wipe fillets with a damp cloth and season with salt, pepper and lemon juice. Place a stalk of asparagus, a raw oyster, a sardine or a piece of lobster on end of each fillet. Roll and fasten with short skewer. Sprinkle with bread crumbs and place a very small piece of butter on each rolled fillet. Cook 20 minutes in moderate oven. Serve with Hollandaise sauce. Other kinds of fillets may be used.

Hollandaise Sauce:

½ cup butter
2-4 egg yolks
¼ tsp. salt
  cayenne to taste
½ cup boiling water
  juice of ½ lemon

Cream butter; add egg yolk one at a time, beating thoroughly. Add seasonings and water, and cook in double boiler, beating constantly until thick. Add lemon juice last.

Serves 4.

Mrs. Cecilia M. Clairmont, Arcadia, N.S.

STUFFED FISH STEAKS

6 fish steaks (cod or haddock)
lemon juice
salt
pepper
bread stuffing (see below)
melted butter

Select 6 fish steaks of equal size. (If frozen fish steaks, thaw before preparing.) Arrange three fish steaks in a greased, shallow baking dish. Sprinkle with lemon juice, salt and pepper. Spread each steak with bread stuffing and cover with one of the remaining steaks. Brush with melted butter. Bake in a quick moderate oven (375°) for 30 minutes, basting frequently with melted butter. Serve with lemon wedges.

Bread Stuffing:

Melt 3 tbsp. butter.
Add 2 tbsp. chopped onions,
and ⅓ cup finely chopped celery.

Cook above until tender but not brown. Add to 1½ cups day old bread crumbs and mix well. Season with ½ tsp. salt, ⅛ tsp. pepper, and ½ tsp. thyme, sage or savoury seasoning. If stuffing is too dry, add 2 tbsp. of water or milk.

Serves 6.

Muriel Horton, Canso, N.S.

FISH SOUFFLÉ

4 oz. any cooked flaked fish
2 oz. butter
2 oz. flour
½ pint fish stock or milk
2 eggs (separated)
seasoning
browned bread crumbs

Make a cream sauce with butter, flour and liquid. Pour this on slightly beaten egg yolks. Add fish. Whip the egg whites until stiff and fold into mixture. Put into a soufflé dish, season and dust with browned bread crumbs. Bake in hot oven for ½ hour.

Serves 4.

Mrs. Charles H. Sutherland, Halifax, N.S.

SUPERB FISH STEAKS

4 white fish steaks
2 tbsp. butter
1 clove of garlic
salt
2 tbsp. flour
4 tbsp. apple juice
4 tbsp. water
pepper

Topping:

1 small onion (chopped)
½ pint mushrooms (sliced)
½ green pepper (chopped)
2 tomatoes (cut into eighths)
2 slices white bread (crumbed)
1 tbsp. olive oil
1 tbsp. parsley (chopped)

Set oven to 400°. Melt butter and bruise garlic. Sauté garlic and salt in butter. Stir in flour and add juice and water to make a sauce. Add pepper to taste. Pour over steaks in shallow dish. Sauté onion, mushrooms, green pepper and tomatoes in olive oil. Stir in bread crumbs and parsley. Spread over steaks in dish. Cover and bake 25-30 minutes, removing cover for final 5 minutes.

Serves 2-4.

Susan Bagley, Tantallon, N.S.

ROLLED FISH

- 2 lbs. fish fillets (ocean perch, halibut or cod)
- 1 lb. broccoli, asparagus or spinach (cooked)
  vinaigrette sauce (see below)

Divide cooked broccoli among fillets. Roll up. Secure with toothpicks. Arrange in greased 8 cup baking dish. Pour on vinaigrette sauce and bake at 350° for 20 minutes while basting often.

Vinaigrette Sauce:

- 1 Oxo onion cube
- ¾ cup boiling water
- 1 tsp. salt
- ¼ tsp. paprika
- ½ cup vegetable oil
- ¼ cup cider vinegar
- ¼ cup chopped sour pickles
- 2 tbsp. brown sugar
- 1 tbsp. parsley flakes

Dissolve onion cube in boiling water. Add remaining ingredients. Bring to boil. Reduce heat and simmer 10 minutes. Serve hot or cold.

Serves 5-6.

Mrs. Ethel Higgins, Dartmouth, N.S.

ANGELS ON HORSE-BACK

- 1 lb. smoked fillets of any kind
  pepper to taste
  butter
- 2 eggs (poached)

Steam fillets in usual way. Drain. Place knob of butter and poached egg on each portion. Serve with fresh bread and salad. Great for lunch.

Serves 2.

Daphne Hogan, Chester, N.S.

SMOKED FILLETS SUPREME

- 1½ lbs. smoked fillets
- 1½ tbsp. flour
- 1 small onion
- 1½ cups milk
- 2 tbsp. butter

Place smoked fillets in saucepan and cover with cold water. Bring fish to boiling point. Then drain. Place fish in bottom of baking dish; sprinkle each layer of fish with flour. Slice onion in thin slices and place on top of fillets. Dot with pieces of butter, then add milk. Bake 15 to 20 minutes in hot oven (450°).

Serves 4.

Miss Muriel Horton, Canso, N.S.

GRAN'MA'S SALT HERRING AND POTATOES

- 1 large or 2 medium salted herring
- 5 or 6 large potatoes

Soak herring overnight in water to freshen. Next day, wash unpeeled potatoes thoroughly and boil in their skins in a large pot (one with room enough for the fish later). About ten minutes before the potatoes are done, lay whole drained fish on top and cook remaining 10 minutes. Serve hot, with butter melting on top. This is especially good with a side dish of sliced cucumbers in sour cream.

Serves 4-6.

Kay Hill, Ketch Harbour, N.S.

FRIED GASPEREAUX OR SHAD

2 lbs. gaspereaux or shad (cleaned)
bacon fat
salt and pepper to taste

Using a "spider" (heavy cast iron fry pan), melt enough bacon fat to cover the bottom. Add fish and sprinkle with salt and pepper to taste. Fry and turn fish until done or flaky. Do not overcook.

Serves 4.

Mrs. Bettie M. Parker, Economy, N.S.

DIPPING GASPEREUAX

The Gaspereaux River Valley in Kings County, Nova Scotia was settled in 1755 and received its name from the abundance of gaspereaux, which the English called "alewives". Gaspereaux are still caught easily with the use of long handled dip-nets, and fishermen dip the fish from "dipping" platforms constructed along the river. The gaspereaux are often salted and packed in barrels right on the spot.

BAKED GASPEREAUX OR SHAD

2 lbs. gaspereaux or shad (cleaned)
butter, salt and pepper to taste
lemon juice (optional)

Place fish in a shallow greased baking dish. Dot with butter. Add pepper, salt and lemon juice to taste. Bake in 350° oven for 30 minutes.

Serves 4.

Mrs. Bettie M. Parker, Economy, N.S.

An Intriguing Sight – Dipping the Spring Run of Gaspereaux.

PORT MAITLAND SPECIAL (BAKED MACKEREL)

1 large fresh mackerel
pepper and salt to taste
2 tbsp. butter

Split fish, clean, remove head and tail. Place skin down in a well buttered baking pan. (I prefer to line the pan with foil.) Sprinkle lightly with salt and pepper. Dot with butter. Allow 2 tablespoons to a large sized fish.

Sauce:

½ cup brown sugar
¼ cup apple cider vinegar

Mix well. Carefully baste fish with sauce before placing in 400° oven. Bake for 20 minutes. Baste two more times with remaining sauce while baking.

Serves 4.

Geraldine Ellis Gates, Weymouth, N.S.

FRIED MACKEREL — WITH BLACK BUTTER SAUCE

fresh mackerel fillets — at least two per person
milk
pancake flour
¼ cup butter
1 tbsp. vinegar
some capers or chopped onion

Dip fillets in milk, then in pancake flour. Fry in deep fat until brown. Set aside and keep hot. Melt butter in skillet until a deep brown. Add chopped capers (onion can be substituted) and vinegar. Mix well. Place hot fillets on hot serving plates and pour sauce over them. Serve immediately.

Viola P. Hollett, Granville Ferry, N.S.

BAKED CREAMED MACKEREL

4 mackerel fillets or 2 whole, cleaned mackerel
2 large onions
salt, pepper to taste
1½ cups Blend
flour, butter

Roll mackerel in flour, salt and pepper. Lay fish in a flat pan or small roaster, cut side up. Slice onion over fish and dot with butter. Pour Blend over fish to almost cover. Bake in 400° oven for 30 minutes. Serve with mashed potatoes, peas and carrots.

Serves 4.

Evelyn Bonn,
Musquodoboit Harbour, N.S.

SOUSED MACKEREL

5 or 6 mackerel, cleaned and cut in serving-sized pieces
1 tbsp. salt (scant)
½ tsp. sugar (more if desired)
2 tbsp. pickling spice tied in cheese cloth
1 cup vinegar
½ cup water
sliced onion if desired

Put fish in deep baking dish. Cover with salt, sugar, vinegar, water and onion. Put spices in cheese cloth bag in centre. Bake in a 350° oven uncovered for at least 2 hours. Very good hot or as a cold snack.

Serves 6-8.

Enid L. Germain, Yarmouth, N.S.

Beautiful Rivers and Streams of the Margaree Valley Provide Excellent Salmon and Trout Fishing.

TROUT TIPS

Trout must be kept clean, dry and cool (storing it in moss is good while in the woods). Frying trout in butter with freshly ground pepper is best. Remember they curl up when freshly cooked so tend them carefully.

For a change, try cooking a few mushrooms in butter; add parsley and bread crumbs. Then stuff the trout. Sprinkle with white wine and bake 10 minutes on each side in a hot oven. Serve with new potatoes rolled in chives and fresh pot greens.

Trout may also be steamed on a bed of mint. Delicious when cooled.

Joan Czapalay

STEWED EELS

2 lbs. eels (small family)
5 lbs. eels (large family)
1 medium turnip (diced)
2 large onions (sliced)
    (if for large family, double the vegetables)

Place all together in pot; add two cups of water. Do not cover eels as they will make water. Simmer for 1½ hours. Simmering brings out the flavor. Serve with mashed potatoes and any vegetable you wish.

Evelyn Bonn,
Musquodoboit Harbour, N.S.

STUFFED BAKED STRIPED BASS

   1 (4 or 5 lb.) bass, cleaned
      salt (and pepper if desired)
   ¼ cup butter
   1 cup chopped onion
   ½ cup thinly sliced celery
   4 cups bread crumbs
   ½ tsp. sage (or to taste)
   2 tbsp. lemon juice
   2 strips of bacon

Preheat oven to 350°. Sprinkle bass inside and out with salt. In a skillet heat ¼ cup butter. Add onion, celery and cook until tender. Mix with bread crumbs, herbs and lemon juice. Stuff bass loosely with bread mixture; close with skewers and string. Place on a foil-lined baking dish. Brush bass with more melted butter and place bacon over top. Bake until the fish flakes easily, about 35 to 40 minutes. Baste with butter as necessary. Serve with lemon butter.
Serves 6.
   Mrs. Mildred Vitiello, Port Royal, N.S.

BAKED FILLET OF STRIPED BASS

   2 lbs. filleted striped bass
   4 tbsp. good cooking oil
   2 medium sized onions
   1 (19 oz) can of tomatoes
      seasoning to taste

Cut bass into serving sized pieces and place in oiled baking dish. Add sliced onion over fish. Pour contents of 19 oz. can of tomatoes over fish. Bake in 350° oven until fish flakes. Add water as necessary to prevent sticking. Serve with broccoli and boiled potatoes.
Serves 6.
   Anonymous, Granville Ferry, N.S.

Fishing for Striped Bass on the Annapolis River.

BAKED EELS

eels
dry mustard
salt and pepper to taste

Skin and remove insides from eels; be sure they are well blooded. Soak in cold water for one hour. (This will remove all blood.) Slit down the sides and remove fins and tail. Cut into 2″ pieces. Place in a large baking pan or large cookie sheet with sides to retain the fat. Shake dry mustard, salt and pepper to taste over them. Bake at 425° for 1 to 1½ hours or until the top is crispy brown. Serve with your favorite vegetables and tossed salad. NOTE: Cut eels in smaller pieces, bake and serve as hors d'oeuvres with crackers. Excellent!

Evelyn Bonn,
Musquodoboit Harbour, N.S.

FRIED SMELTS

Roll cleaned smelts in mixture of half flour and half cornmeal. Fry fish in cooking oil or bacon fat (enough to cover the bottom of fry pan) until nicely browned on both sides. Do not overcook as they will break apart easily. Salt and pepper to taste. The backbone removes very easily when you open smelt and lift it out slowly from one end.

STRIPED BASS FISHING

The Annapolis River has long been a popular spot for bass fishermen. A dam with a causeway was constructed at the eastern end of the Annapolis Basin, but a fishway continues to allow the fish to travel the river without hindrance.

SEAFOOD SUPREME

1 cup fresh scallops
1 cup fresh halibut
1 cup fresh or frozen shrimp
1 cup fresh or frozen lobster
  milk

Scald 1 cup of scallops in 1 cup of salted water for 5 minutes. Drain and save liquid. Heat slowly 1 cup halibut, 1 cup shrimp and 1 cup lobster also for 5 minutes. Save liquid from all fish.

Sauce:
1 cup sliced mushrooms
½ onion (sliced)
3 tbsp. pimento (chopped)
3 tbsp. green pepper (chopped)
¼ tsp. prepared mustard
6 tbsp. flour
6 tbsp. butter
1 cup Blend
  Worcestershire sauce to taste

Add enough milk to fish broth to make 2 cups. Melt 6 tbsp. butter in large saucepan; add flour and blend carefully. Then stir milk and fish broth in slowly until thickened. Add mushrooms, onion, green pepper, and pimento. Also add Worcestershire sauce to taste, and ¼ tsp. prepared mustard. Last of all add Blend. Then add fish and let simmer slowly for 15-20 min. to blend flavors. Serve on bed of fluffy rice.

Serves 8-10.

Iva Wood, Halifax, N.S.

LOBSTER À LA NEWBURG

1 pint cooked lobster meat (diced)
1 cup cream
2 egg yolks (beaten)
4 tbsp. butter
½ tbsp. flour
1 tsp. lemon juice
salt and paprika

Melt 3 tbsp. butter in saucepan, and in this heat the diced lobster. In another saucepan melt the other tbsp. butter; then stir in flour and cook. Add the cream, whisking until it is smooth; when at the boiling point draw aside from heat and add the beaten egg yolks, stirring as it thickens. Then add the lobster, seasonings and lemon juice. When very hot serve with slices of thin dry toast, or toasted crackers. Do not boil again after adding egg yolks or mixture will curdle.

Serves 5-6.

E. B. Higgins, Dartmouth, N.S.

FRIED LOBSTER

2 cups cooked lobster
2 eggs
2 tbsp. butter
salt and pepper

Beat 2 eggs until fluffy. Dip cooked lobster in egg mixture and place in frying pan in which 2 tbsp. of butter have been melted. Sprinkle with salt and pepper and fry lightly until golden brown.

Serves 4.

Betty Hardiman, Port Hawkesbury, N.S.

CRABS — SEAQUEEN STYLE

12 large crabs
1 tbsp. butter
3 tbsp. of flour
1 cup of cream
1 tsp. of parsley
3 sieved, hard-cooked egg yolks
1 tsp. of H.P. sauce
salt and pepper
bread crumbs, buttered

Cover crabs with boiling hot water and simmer for 20 minutes. Drain; break off all claws; separate the shells and discard spongy parts under shell. Remove meat. Clean the upper shells of the crabs thoroughly and set aside for filling. Melt butter in a saucepan. Blend in the flour and heat the mixture until it bubbles. Remove from heat; gradually add cream, stirring constantly. Continue stirring and cook for 2 minutes until the sauce is thick. Mix in the parsley, sieved egg yolks, seasoning and crab meat. Fill the shells with this mixture and top with bread crumbs. Bake at 350° for 10 minutes until the bread crumbs are browned lightly.

Serves 4.

Mrs. Olive Roy, Halifax, N.S.

Bluenose II – Pride of Nova Scotia. The Original Bluenose was Queen of the North Atlantic Fishing Fleet.

OYSTER PIE

1 pint (about 24) oysters, or 2 (7 oz) cans

½ cup onions, sautéed in 2 tsp. butter

Pie shell:

  2 cups flour

  1 tsp. salt

  ⅔ cup lard

  ¼ cup water

Thick White Sauce:

  ¼ cup butter

  ¼ cup flour

  ¼ tsp. salt

  ⅛ tsp. pepper

  1 cup milk

Make standard pie pastry and line pie plate. Make standard *thick* white sauce. Avoid lumps by allowing flour and butter one minute removed from heat before adding 1 cup milk. Be sure to stir continually until sauce thickens. Sauté ½ cup onions in butter. Combine all ingredients with oysters and pour into pie shell. Cover with remaining pastry. Cook at 400° for ½ hour until it tests done.

Serves 4-6.

  Deian Hartwell, Shearwater, N.S.

FRIED OYSTERS

  oysters (3-4 per person)

1 egg (beaten)

  cracker crumbs

  butter, or cooking oil

Clean oysters and dry with paper towel. Dip in slightly beaten egg and roll in cracker crumbs. Brown all over in butter, or other fat, in hot frypan.

  Frances Goudey, Yarmouth, N.S.

BAKED SCALLOPS IN HALF SHELL

8-10 scallops (per person)
    potato slices
  1 tbsp. milk or cream
    salt and pepper to taste
    cracker crumbs
    butter
    lemon slices

Clean scallop shells in warm, soapy water; rinse well. Slice each scallop meat in half. In each shell place several thin slices of potato, 3 to 4 scallop slices, 1 tbsp. milk or cream, salt and pepper to taste. Sprinkle each shell with finely crushed cracker crumbs and put a small piece of butter on each. Bake in oven at 400° until well browned and potatoes are tender. Serve with lemon slices. For each person allow 4 to 5 filled shells.

    Mary Anne Turner, Lockeport, N.S.

FRIED SCALLOPS

6-8 scallops (per person)
    butter
    salt and pepper

Wipe scallops with a damp cloth. Fry in butter until a golden brown. Turn and brown on other side. Season both sides with salt and pepper.

    Mrs. Emily Lohnes, Bridgewater, N.S.

The Famous Digby Scallop Fleet – One of the Largest in the World.

CLAM FRITTERS

1 lb. chopped or whole clams
1 cup milk or part clam juice
1 tbsp. melted butter
2 beaten eggs
1 cup flour
1 tsp. baking powder
   salt and pepper to taste
   enough oil to cover bottom of frying pan

Beat milk, butter, and eggs. Mix flour, baking powder and seasonings; add to milk mixture slowly, blending until smooth. Add clams gradually to batter. Drop in hot oil in frying pan. Flip after 3 minutes and fry to a golden brown.

Serves 6, depending on appetites.

Shirley Hines, Head of Chezzetcook, N.S.

STEAMED CLAMS

Fresh clams will "spit" or clean themselves when left in a bucket of fresh water for about an hour. Remove clams from fresh water and rinse in the sink. Scrub any that appear sandy. Add clams to a large pot and fill about half full with fresh water. Add salt to taste. Steam for 20 minutes or until clams open. Drain and serve with cups of strained clam broth, drawn butter and vinegar for "dipping".

DIGBY SCALLOP FLEET

The boats of the famous Digby Scallop Fleet are specially designed for work in the scallop beds. They must be well built to operate in the Atlantic Ocean since their daily travel exposes them to some very rough weather. Delicious Digby scallops are enjoyed all over the world.

SUPER SEAFOOD SUPPER

2 (283.5 g or 10 oz) tins mushrooms
4 (10 oz) tins condensed cream of shrimp soup (frozen type if possible)
1 cup light cream
4 tbsp. butter or margarine
8-10 cups cut up, cooked seafood (2 tins drained, cleaned shrimp, 2 lbs. scallops, 2 tins lobster meat)
1 cup grated cheddar cheese
¾ cup sauterne, if desired

Drain mushrooms and brown lightly in butter in a large saucepan. Add soup and cream. Heat slowly. Cut scallops in pieces and simmer in a small amount of water. Add liquid with scallops to mixture (approximately 1 cup liquid). Blend in remainder of seafood, and cheese, and stir over low heat until cheese is melted. Add sauterne just before serving. Ladle over patty shells.

Serves 25.

Mrs. D.L. Chipman, Yarmouth, N.S.

PLANKED SALMON

This is a Micmac Indian method still practised by the Queens County Guides Association and the Greenfield Fire Department.

- 1 hardwood plank (2½"x17"x36")
- 2 hardwood pieces (2½"x2½"x48")
- 26 (2½") galvanized nails
- 4 (4") galvanized nails

Drill and nail as per illustration below, with 2½" nails raised enough for lacing on the salmon.

- 20 cement blocks, around campfire
- 2 empty gallon tins
- 1 coil of wire
- ½ cord split hardwood (24" lengths)
- 20 lbs. charcoal briquettes
  wide aluminum foil
- 1 (8-10 lb.) salmon
  peppercorns and sea salt to taste
- 2 dozen ears of corn
- 2½ lbs. butter (melted)
  cole slaw for 6 to 8 people

At least two hours before cooking, build fire to heat backing of cement blocks per illustration and provide radiant heat. Add charcoal before cooking time.

Scale and split salmon at back to remove back bone, fins and entrails. Lay salmon on aluminum foil on plank, skin side down between nails, and lace with wire. (Indians secured fish with green withes which were heat resistant). Season with sea salt and ground pepper. Then dredge with melted butter.

Place planked salmon in front of fire with 2½" pieces of wood in tins filled with water to prevent burning. Have a pail of water handy for same purpose. Have a cement block to support the plank at a proper angle for intense heat to cook fish. Continually baste with butter. When one side is cooked, reverse and test for doneness. Serve with corn on the cob and cole slaw. Plan to reserve plank for future use.

Serves 6 to 8.

Donald and Marion MacKay,
Hirtle's Beach, N.S.

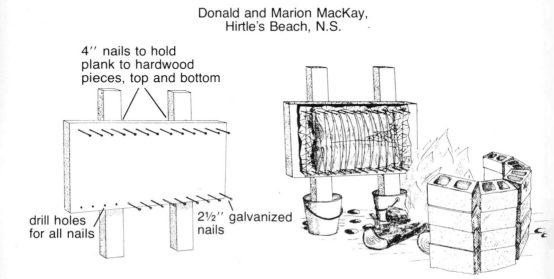

4" nails to hold plank to hardwood pieces, top and bottom

drill holes for all nails

2½" galvanized nails

Picturesque Glace Bay Harbour, with Colourful Boats and Lobster Pots.

HERRING BONELESS

A versatile recipe for snacks, luncheon or supper.

- 2 herrings
- 2 hard boiled eggs
- 2 small onions
- 1 tsp. vinegar
- 1 apple (2 carrots are a good substitute)
- 1 tsp. anchovy essence (optional)
- 6 drops of Tabasco sauce
- 1 tbsp. of butter

  pepper and salt, if the herring is fresh or frozen.

Clean, fillet and skin herrings (an art in itself, so it's best to have the fishmonger do it for you.) Chop fish into small chunks. If the herring is fresh, begin preparation. If frozen, thaw and continue. Soak salted fish overnight and change the water.

Herring which has been soaked in brine may be used as is, but please note that it is then unnecessary to sauté.

Sauté onions and chopped herring in 1 tbsp. of butter. Place cored and peeled apple with hard-boiled eggs in mixer and chop. Add sautéed herring and onion. Add vinegar, pepper, salt, Tabasco and anchovy essence. Run mixer at chop speed or mix well by hand. At this stage a busy hostess may wish to store the mixture in the refrigerator until required.

Suggested Servings:

To serve hot — place the mixture in ramekin dishes and sprinkle wheat germ, bread crumbs or mashed potato over tops. Heat for 10 minutes in a 300 degree oven. Then grill briefly until tops are a golden brown. Serve immediately.

To serve cold — serve directly from the refrigerator on lettuce leaves with cucumber. Top with bean sprouts and creamed salad dressing.

Serves 2.

Anonymous

BRILLED LOBSTER

7 live chicken lobsters (1 to 1¼ lbs. each; at least 3 female, and if one-claw have crusher claw)

1½-2 lbs. butter or margarine (melted)

2 lbs. or quarts toasted bread crumbs

individual dishes for melted butter

lobster shears or nut crackers, and lobster forks

The following procedure is easier when performed on live lobsters, and if you do not want to do it yourself, ask your fish dealer to do it for you shortly before brilling. Alternatively, the lobsters may be boiled for 2 to 5 minutes beforehand.

Place lobster with claws up on cutting board and split through to back shell from point in illustration to end of tail portion using sharp pointed knife. With scissors or lobster shears, cut top shell to point between claws, being careful not to perforate the stomach sac or lady. Separate body with thumbs and with fingers under sac, remove it and discard. Cut "V" in tail and remove intestinal tract.

Stuffing:

Have a large bowl half filled with toasted bread crumbs and add liquid, liver and tamale from body. Reserve portion of roe to sauté in butter and when turned red add to crumbs. Repeat with remaining lobsters and gently blend in crumbs, adding half of heated butter. Spread cavity and mound up with stuffing. Baste with melted butter over crumbs to prevent burning.

Place lobsters on broiling pan in preheated oven, 500 to 550 degrees and brill (bake-broil) 15 to 20 minutes. To test, remove tail portion of one of the lobsters allowing each guest a piece to dip in hot melted butter. Serve remaining six lobsters on a platter. Toss a fresh salad including tomatoes, lettuce, cucumbers, sliced mushrooms, cubed cheddar cheese, peppers, Spanish onions and your choice of dressing.
Serves 6.

Donald and Marion MacKay,
Hirtle's Beach, N.S.

Top view
of lobster

These two procedures **must**
be performed on the
underside of the lobster:

with scissors or lobster
shears split and sever
spinal cord

with sharp pointed
knife cut
top shell

Fishy Facts (Helpful Hints)

1. Fresh fish should have firm flesh which springs back when dented with fingers. If fish is truly fresh, it should be odourless and free of slime; however, salt water fish will smell like the sea from which it came.

2. Fish is so nutritious that it has often been called "brain food". It is found to be high in protein, the B vitamins, and many minerals. Salt water fish provides an excellent source of iodine. Fish is also a low-cholesterol food.

3. Fish should never be over-cooked. It is "done" when it flakes easily with a fork or comes away from the bones without too much resistance. When fish is over-cooked it becomes dry and loses its flavour.

4. White fish may be used in many of the same recipes. Haddock, halibut, sole, cod, flounder, plaice, turbot and perch are examples of the "white fish".

5. When cooking frozen fish, thaw in refrigerator (never at room temperature) in its original package for approximately six hours per pound. Use immediately after thawing or store in fridge up to 24 hours only. Never re-freeze.

6. Uncooked fresh fish may be stored in the freezer for three to six months.

7. Fresh fish may be stored in refrigerator for two days without freezing.

8. Using seashells and your imagination, create your own shellcrafts and fun. An entertaining hobby!

9. Dried salted fish can be freshened when soaked in cold fresh water overnight; drained; covered with water again; simmered slowly and drained again. If fish is still too salty for your taste, re-cover with fresh cold water and simmer again until satisfactory.

A Typical Fishing Community found along Nova Scotia's Coastline.

10. Any cooked, leftover fish may be used in salads, sandwiches, chowders and hors d'oeuvres. Just use your imagination!

11. Fish odour may be removed from the hands by washing them with salt and water.

12. Mix a tin of lobster paste in your fish chowder before serving for a gourmet touch.

13. Poached salmon may be cooked to correct "doneness" by inserting a meat thermometer into the center of the salmon and cooking to the exact temperature of 155°. This is especially helpful when using frozen fish.

14. Dried salted fish can be stored in the lower part of refrigerator. If kept cold and dry in an air-tight wrapper or container, you can store this fish for several months until needed. This fish is ideal for camping trips too.

15. In recipes calling for fish that has to be handled a lot (fishcakes), use dried salted fish. Since the process hardens the fish, it is therefore easier to handle and won't break apart too easily.

16. Remember that all smoked fish has been *salted* to a certain degree first. Test your recipe before adding more salt.

17. Add many nutrients to your garden soil by working in any sea shells. They are especially good for roses.

Liverpool – From 1800-1812 Privateers Sailed from Here in Search of Plunder.

Index

Index